Handbook
for Ministers
of Care

Second Edition

Genevieve Glen, OSB

Marilyn Kofler, SP

Kevin O'Connor

LITURGY
TRAINING
PUBLICATIONS

Acknowledgments

Scripture quotations from the *New American Bible* © 1970, Confraternity of Christian Doctrine Washington, DC, are used by license of the copyright owner. All rights reserved. No part of the *New American Bible* may be reproduced without permission in writing from the copyright owner.

Excerpts from the English translation of *Pastoral Care of the Sick: Rites of Anointing and Viaticum* © 1982, International Committee on English in the Liturgy, Inc. All rights reserved.

The text on page 64 – 65 is reprinted with permission from PACER Center, 4826 Chicago Avenue South, Minneapolis MN 55417; 612-827-2966.

This book was edited by David Philippart. Audrey Novak Riley was the production editor. It was designed by Anna Manhart and typeset by Karen Mitchell in Goudy. The illustrations are the work of Carolina Arentsen. Printed in the United Sates of America.

Copyright © 1997, Archdiocese of Chicago: Liturgy Training Publications, 3949 South Racine Avenue, Chicago IL 60609; 1-800-933-1800; fax 1-800-933-7094; e-mail orders@ltp.org. All rights reserved. Visit our Web site at www.LTP.org.

Library of Congress Cataloging-in-Publications Data
Glen, Genevieve.
    Handbook for ministers of care / Genevieve Glen, Marilyn Kofler, Kevin O'Connor. — 2nd ed.
        p. cm.
    ISBN 1-56854-102-3
        1. Church work with the sick — Handbooks, manuals, etc.
    2. Pastoral medicine — Catholic Church — Handbooks, manuals, etc.
    I. Kofler, Marilyn. II. O'Connor, Kevin E. III. Title.
    BX2347.S5G57   1997
    259' .4 — dc21   97-28263
                                                                        CIP
ISBN 978-1-56854-102-0
HBMCR2

18 17 16 15 14   7 8 9 10 11

Contents

These prayerbooks published by Liturgy Training Publications will help you in your ministry of care:

Prayers of the Sick

Rites of the Sick

Chapter 1

Called to Minister
with the Sick

You might know some of these people. A very old woman will never leave the nursing home where she has lived for the past eight years. A not so very old man is bedridden from an accident that has left him dependent on others for life. Parents keep vigil for their premature newborn. A woman with beautiful blue eyes is slowly wasted away by disease. A teenager sits alone and afraid in a psychiatric ward. A child with pneumonia ignores the toys that clutter her room.

They are all ordinary people in extraordinary situations. As much as medical attention, they need support and comfort. In a word, they need care. As a minister of care, you visit the sick, the grieving, the aged, the dying. In presence and prayer and sacrament you bring this support and comfort from person to person, uniting the church.

Here's what a parishioner once reported:

> My brother-in-law died a number of years ago and like many good people we all know, he died after a long bout with cancer. During the six months of his illness a special man came to visit — to talk, to listen, to bring communion, and to represent the local parish. His name was Paul.
>
> Paul was an ordinary man, quiet, steady, but very ordinary, a person like you or me. A discouraged and very sad family came to know Paul well. If there was any doubt that Jesus existed, Paul put our doubts to rest. Jesus was here in this very ordinary man. And when death finally came and went, Paul stayed.

In our gospels we proclaim a Lord who suffers with the suffering, who grieves with the grieving, who knows our isolation, our pain. Every Christian is called to the tasks of healing and comforting and companionship. But there are people among us with special gifts, gifts that need recognition within our community. These people can give in the name of the church, in the name of Christ. They can give their gifts in the name of our communities and become the sacramental presence of Christ in our midst.

But ministry is a two-way street. It's never simply "givers" and "receivers," separating the ministers from those to whom they minister. The sick, the grieving, the aged and the dying all have their own gifts to give, for they are signs of Christ suffering and dying in our own flesh and blood. In their troubled minds and bodies the Lord Jesus is alive. Ministers of care will always be given more than they can give.

As a minister of care, you are commissioned by your parish to bring the compassion and communion of the church to the sick and the homebound. But you also have a commission to bear witness to the parish at large: to bring before the whole community the suffering of its members, the suffering of Christ. You become "gift bearers" from parishioner to parishioner, distributing the gifts of the Spirit to each according to need.

Ministers of care are ordinary people called to minister to ordinary people in extraordinary circumstances. This book is written to help these ordinary people develop their gifts as they seek to become ministers of care.

A Parish Ministry

"I wonder what it's like to be a minister of care. It must take a special person to be able to deal with so much illness and pain." "I've never prayed with another person out loud." "Nursing homes really frighten me."

"Bringing communion to the elderly is something I've always wanted to do. I really want to visit people in nursing homes, but I'm not sure I'd feel comfortable visiting patients in a hospital." "I just couldn't visit cancer patients — but I'd like to visit others!"

"I'd be good with women and children, but I'm not so sure about visiting men." "I work all day, but I could visit on my lunch hour."

"I've been in and out of hospitals myself and I know how lonely and frightening serious illness can be. A minister of care visited me — and I'd like to be like her." "Prayer has always been important in my life. I'd like to share that with others." "My father died of cancer. I'd like to help others like him." "I'd really like to be a minister of care, but I don't know if I have what it takes."

Each person responds differently to the call to be a minister of care. Every response is colored by experience. Such feelings, fears and hopes need to be aired in a process of discernment, that is, in shared reflection with one who is already part of this ministry.

An initial interview with the coordinator or supervisor of a parish's ministry of care revolves around the question: "How do I know this is for me?" Ordinarily, the interview will include much listening to the newcomer: his or her hopes and expectations, experiences of illness, of the elderly and of death. The prospective minister will have questions that need to be answered: How much time will this ministry take? How will I know what to do? How do I know I can do a good job? The coordinator will discuss the specific goals of the ministry of care, the training and ongoing enrichment involved, the expected time commitment. The interview itself is the opportunity for both the prospective minister and the coordinator to discern a commitment to the training program and involvement in this ministry.

Most training programs include at least six two-hour sessions that focus on ministry, basic skills for pastoral visitation, the experience of illness, the aging process, death and dying, prayer and pastoral visitation, and eucharistic ministry to the sick. At the conclusion of the training program the new ministers of care are commissioned, usually at a Sunday Mass in the parish.

Ongoing formation and supervision are very important to nourish and sustain the ministers of care. A two-hour session held once a month provides continuing formation, offers an opportunity for reflection on experiences, becomes a forum to discuss questions and problems and is the occasion for peer support, shared prayer and growth in ministry. Business is kept to a minimum at these sessions.

Once a year, it is important to gather and look at the original goals, expectations and commitments, and to evaluate them in light of the experiences of the individual ministers of care.

There is more information on initial training and ongoing formation in the appendix of this book.

Is this a lifetime commitment? No. It is acceptable and even expected to "retire" or go on to a different form of ministry at some point. The expected commitment of a minister of care can be for one, two or three years. When the period of commitment comes to a close, it is important that the minister and supervisor take time together to discern whether to renew the commitment.

The Person

Ministry of care is one of the oldest ministries in the church. It was a ministry open to all the baptized that gradually, through the ages, became a ministry for priests and religious, especially those who established and served in hospitals. The renewal of this ministry among all who are baptized is one of the many good works to come from Vatican II. The ministry of care thrives today as people within the community minister to one another's needs.

It has become clear to many in parish work that the pastoral care of the sick, the elderly and the dying requires not only serious commitment from the parish, but the presence of carefully trained volunteers with professional direction.

This ministry is a powerful witness to God's presence. It is a service to others that is humbling and at times frustrating, but it is a significant means of sharing in Christ's healing power. This ministry is both a sign of hope and an intimate sharing of the good news.

The Prayer

Ministers of care know from experience about two forms of praying.

Prayers from tradition are one form. The "Our Father" is such a prayer. So are the psalms and many hymns and songs. So is the rite of communion for the sick and for the dying. These prayers allow us to join our voices to the whole church. When we repeat them again and again, when we memorize them, they become alive in us. They are one way we give to our own lives the very shape of the gospel. They say something important about how we feel, and about what we want to be.

There is also a kind of prayer that allows us to hear. This is the prayer of listening. It is listening to the spirit, recognizing God's movement and words in our lives.

Ritual prayer and prayer-as-listening are both life-giving activities. They are responses in faith to our position in the world, to our belief about ourselves and to our belief about God.

Frequently, in your ministry, you may find yourself centering on prayers of petition. With some conscious effort to find other dimensions in prayer, you can praise, bless and thank God and also express the sorrow and desire for forgiveness that is deep in Christian life.

Ministers of care gradually learn how broad and many-sided, yet how simple, prayer is. You will become at home with prayer as thanksgiving, prayer as petition, prayer as praise, prayer as sorrow.

The Presence

Your presence is who you are more than what you say or do. You know this from experience. You can look back at certain people who have entered your life and lifted you: perhaps a family member or someone you knew only briefly. Ministers of care are people who provide that kind of presence.

We cannot make any once-and-for-all lists of what it takes to have such a presence to others. You may be able to think of people who were encouraging to you, people who gave you hope, people who allowed you to see how you needed to come to grips with yourself, people who saw something that was inside you and brought it forth.

The Purpose

First, you are a representative of your faith community. You are to be yourself, but to be from others. You come to a particular person in faith to witness that the faith is alive in your local community, that these Christians truly do love one another.

Second, you are to engage this person in a relationship. You are seeking something like the saving relationship that helped people come to know Jesus through faith. In his relationships, Jesus did four things for people. He gave them life, he encouraged them, he showed great trust in them and he released them to themselves. Those whom Jesus touched never became dependent on him. Through a saving kind of relationship with them, he released them.

This is the real key to ministry of care. You need to create a relationship as Jesus did. You need to give life and to encourage and develop the kind of relationship that allows people to trust themselves, to trust you, to trust the Lord.

Third, you are a prayerful example of God's presence. You stand before a person in great need saying, "God wants you to come close." You are also an example of personal faith: In your work as a minister of care, you demonstrate what God's presence in your life means to you.

Chapter 2

Understanding Sickness and Healing

Before we minister to the sick in the name of Jesus Christ, we need to spend a little time reflecting on sickness and healing in the light of the gospel. Otherwise, we may find that what we say to those we visit comes either from the views prevalent in our society, unconditioned by the good news of God's saving love, or from our own limited experiences. Society's views and our own experiences may reflect profound truth, but they also may be narrower than the full Christian understanding of this mystery.

Sickness

"Suffering and illness have always been among the greatest problems that trouble the human spirit." (PCS, 1) Job — not the patient Job of the book's opening chapter but the bitter, angry Job of the later chapters — demanded from God the explanation many of us seek: If God is loving and all-powerful, why do good people suffer? Job, braver than most of us, put God on trial to defend the truth of the divine love and the divine power in face of the inescapable fact that good people do suffer. Job got an answer, but not the one he expected. He met in the whirlwind a God who cannot be held accountable to the limited rules of our human logic, because this is a God whose love and whose power far exceed our small point of view. Before this Mystery, Job fell silent. However, Job's silence, and God's, has not stopped every succeeding generation from asking the questions that plague us all: Why sickness? why suffering? why this person?

No one can presume to supply the answers that God does not provide. However, it is clear that sickness belongs to the disordered world that owes its origin to sin. In the first 11 chapters of the book of Genesis, sin acts like a crack in the mirror of creation. Humanity, created as a couple in the divine image, makes a disastrous choice which results immediately in the severing of the bonds which held human life together: the bond between humanity and God, the bond between the man and the woman, the bond between this human couple and their creative acts of child-bearing and care for the earth. The crack spreads outward from this center in the next generation as brother kills brother, sons mock their father, human ambition builds a tower toward heaven and is cast back to earth, no longer able to communicate in a common tongue. Wherever the human whole is broken, evil is seen to be at work, however anonymously.

Sickness entails just such division. As you may know from personal experience, when you are sick, you find that you're "not yourself." The body, ordinarily taken for granted, becomes the center of attention. It may seem to be an enemy or a prison, not part of you at all. Emotions may feel tangled, with anger, grief or depression taking control at unexpected moments. The sick person loses a sense of personal wholeness. Similarly, relationships between the sick person and friends or relatives who are well may break down. Communication can become difficult between the world of sickness and the world of health. Roles shift as a parent needs care from a child, or an independent person from strangers. People who are sick lose their ordinary place in the daily life of home or workplace, perhaps temporarily, perhaps for good. Relationships with God may become strained as people who are sick or those close to them become angry with God, or feel guilty before God, or find themselves unable to pray in their accustomed ways. Every dimension of the human whole may disintegrate. Chaos threatens. The hand of evil is apparent.

However, the church is quick to make a distinction, quoting Jesus' own answer to those who wanted to know whose sin had caused the blindness of the nameless "man born blind." (See John 9:1 – 7.) Illness in general may be a result of the "crack in the mirror" that owes its origin to sin, but the particular illness of a particular person cannot and must not be interpreted as a punishment due to personal sin. Sick people often feel guilty because they fear that they have brought their illness upon themselves by poor health habits, or because they are no longer able to make their normal contribution to the world around them. It may be true that the illness is the direct result of some ill-considered behavior in the past. Consequence and punishment are not, however, the same thing. We need to be careful not to imply in any way that the illness is a punishment for sin. In fact, we are explicitly forbidden by the gospel of Jesus Christ from passing such judgments on one another. (See Matthew 7:1–5.)

Moreover, we must distinguish between sickness itself, which is always undesirable, and the benefit sick people may draw from their suffering for themselves and for others. Sickness is not, in itself, a good. PCS states emphatically in several places that individuals, the medical profession and all who care for the sick must do everything in their power to fight the illness and to restore sick people to health. Ministers sometimes think that they can help sick people or those around them to grow in holiness by encouraging them to resign themselves to the sickness as a gift from God, or to be grateful for it as a "blessing in disguise," a lesson from God, or a test that they must somehow pass in order to meet with divine approval. Sufferers can certainly be transformed through their suffering, as we shall see further below. That conversion is indeed a gift from God for which one can be truly grateful. However, sickness itself is not a good to be sought or clung to. It belongs to the reign of evil, not to the reign of God.

Healing

This is why Jesus devoted so much of his public ministry to the work of healing the sick. The constant refrain of all his work was, "The reign of God is at hand" (Mark 1:14–15). In word and action, and above all, in the mystery of the cross, Jesus devoted his being, his life, his ministry to the reign of God. When he healed the sick, it was as if he said, in the most vivid and undeniable way that he could, "Here, this is what the reign of God looks like and feels like. All sickness, all suffering, all chaos disappears in the overwhelming presence of the God who is love. Evil divides and fragments but love unites and makes whole all that is broken." In healing the sick, Jesus cast out the reign of evil in favor of the reign of God.

That is why when Jesus cured the sick, he did more than cure them physically. "He heals the broken-hearted and binds up their wounds." (Psalm 147:3) We might say in modern terms that he affirmed the faith that is challenged by sickness; he offered, through his own death and resurrection, the foundation for the hope that is threatened by the recognition of our own mortality; he made possible, through the gift of the Spirit, the radical love of God and neighbor that seems difficult when suffering tempts us to self-centeredness. (See these readings from PCS, 297: Matthew 8:5–17, Mark 10:46–52, Luke 10:25–37, Acts 13:32–39, Romans 8:18–27, 2 Corinthians 4:16–18.) Further, in healing the sick, he mended their broken families and faith communities, and he called all to conversion and reconciliation with God. It is this entire vast work of healing that Christ continues to carry out through the medical, social and pastoral ministries of the church and even in the larger society.

Ministers sometimes feel that they need to promise a cure in order to bring "good news": "You'll be all right, you'll be up and about soon, you'll see." The sick recognize the lie when it is one. And the wise among them know that God's promises are more honest and more true. Physical health may or may not return. The real good news is that, with or without a cure, in the words of the mystic Julian of Norwich, "all shall be well and all manner of thing shall be well" in the end for those who accept the true healing offered by God, spoken through the mystery of the cross. This true healing is obviously far more than physical cure, although it may begin with or include physical cure. In fact, healing sometimes takes place even when physical cure is impossible. Moreover, the healing offered by Christ is far more than a simple return to things as they were before sickness intruded; it is a transformation wrought by the one who says, "Behold, I make all things new" (Revelation 21:5). When one has tasted or touched the reign of God triumphant in the midst of the very worst of human suffering, one is forever changed.

Perhaps the most significant change brought about by the healing touch of Christ through the ministry of the church is that those who are sick are themselves made healers through the very process of being healed. Again and again, PCS repeats that the sick are not merely passive recipients of ministry: They are themselves called to minister to others. (See 3, 5, for example.) Through their suffering, they are asked to join in communion with Christ to accomplish the saving work of the cross for all humanity. Through their passage from the multi-faceted fragmentation of sickness to conversion in faith, hope and love that is the heart of healing, they bear witness, in the midst of families, friends, church and the healthcare world, to the power of the paschal mystery to transform death into life. They offer a different perspective on life to those who have not yet been forced to question the values, priorities and vision by which they live. They proclaim the challenge of the gospel: The reign of God is at hand whether or not they ever arise from the sickbed. The courageous generosity of the human spirit in the face of adversity speaks even from the very heart of weakness. That is the paradox of the cross — and its glory.

It is this good news, then, not the false platitudes of a society that does its best to wave away the realities of sickness, age and death with the magic wand of "let's pretend that this isn't happening," that the minister of the gospel is called upon to proclaim.

Chapter 3

Basic Skills

Like Job, we all have friends who, with the best of intentions, try to comfort us in times of need. At wakes and funerals, in hospital waiting rooms and at home, these friends often have said the wrong things. And we've done the same to our friends, too. How many times have we heard or said:

"Oh, don't worry, I'm sure it will be okay."
"It's all for the best."
"You're tough, you can take it."
"I guess God just wanted him more than you did."
"She's okay now — you'll be with her soon enough."
"Don't worry, honey, you have a great doctor."
"I just had that operation a while back, and you have
    nothing to worry about."
"She looks so peaceful — they did a great job with her."

Now no one who says these things means them in a bad way. These things are said with the best of intentions, even with love. But this kind of communication is not for the minister of care. Our task is something completely different.

This chapter is about what to do, how to do it, what to say, how to say it. Ministers of care need to be more than friends. In fact, ministers of care often minister with people they did not know previously — people they might not otherwise have as friends.

The hallmark of this ministry can best be summed up by the code "Reliable C.A.R.E."

Reliable: When we rely on someone, we trust him or her. Reliable people do what they say they will do. As a minister of care, do what you say you will do. Be on time, be courteous, be reverent and solidly deliver what you say you promise. Help people to trust.

Credible: You don't need to know everything. You only need to know what *you* know. See yourself as a phone line, not a phone. Help people communicate with their inner selves, with God, with their families, with their parish community. Ministers of care facilitate communication.

Attractive: Dress well, look good, smile, pay attention to how loudly or how softly you are speaking. When you visit, use your natural personality: It is your best tool in this ministry. If you have a tendency to speak too much or too little, or to be a bit too forceful, work on supplying instead what the situation requires. Give yourself.

Responsive: Try to help in ways that you are called upon to help. We can't do everything, but we can do many things. Be open to all the possibilities in your speech and in your manner. Even the twinkle in your eyes can be a form of responsiveness to others in need. Listen and respond: communicate.

Empathic: This is the skill that ministers of care need the most. Being empathic is what gives others the feeling "you understand me." It is not the feeling that "You know how I feel," rather, it is the other's experience that "You may not ever have had this particular feeling, but you understand me." Work to understand.

So do you have to be a psychologist or a counselor to be a minister of care? Not at all. In fact, some mental health professionals find this ministry to be very different from their own jobs. Some even find it to be more difficult as well. But it need not be difficult or even complicated. You don't need to be a counselor; you need to know how to connect with another person in prayerful presence. When Jesus was with the woman at the well, when Jesus was with the blind man, when Jesus was with Lazarus — Jesus was not a psychologist! He was prayerfully present with that one other person. And the other knew it.

A Pastoral Visit

So how do you know how to act and what to say when you visit the sick? It's helpful to distinguish between a social visit and a pastoral one. Friends make social visits — they are important and fine. But ministers make pastoral visits — and that is something very different.

A social visit consists of:

- talking about people, places and events
- maintaining a friendly atmosphere
- sharing mutual stories
- entertaining
- comforting, sometimes by avoiding painful topics.

We all need social visits when we are ill. We enjoy the distraction from our pain. It's fun to talk about the weather, our grandchildren, sports or even the latest neighborhood gossip. Social visits relieve us, refresh us and renew us.

In contrast, a pastoral visit consists of:

- focusing on the sick person's thoughts, feelings, reflections and experiences
- accepting problems as they now exist
- helping the sick person share himself or herself
- comforting through facing and sharing the pain
- nourishing the sick person's relationship with God.

Pastoral visits sometimes are best when we can go to the deeper parts of ourselves — our fears, our hopes, our prayer — and reflect with another person on these most important parts of our lives. C. S. Lewis once wrote, "The only way out is through." Pastoral visits show us a way through.

How do you give this kind of help? One quality you will need might be called quiet patience.

Quiet Patience

If you consider that the people you will visit are surrounded by concerns — physical pain, the welfare of a family, anxiety over the future — it may be easier to see the need for your own quiet patience. A nurse from hospice suggested to a family a way of quiet patience in the last days of the mother's life: "Gather round her bed and pray with your mother. Then be there quietly — play some music softly — and let your mother know you will be there for one another." This nurse opened up to the family a way to enter into the dying process together.

Paul, a minister of care from Beaver Creek, Ohio, is an example of quiet patience. Paul ministered to John, who was suffering from cancer. Paul said very little but was there when needed. He even ate lunch with the family at the bedside. Paul was a certified public accountant, skilled in the science of accounting. He wasn't a psychologist, counselor or social worker. Paul was a minister of care who understood the value of quiet patience. He was there and he waited — prayerfully.

Patience is defined as forbearance, or painstaking care toward others. The focus is on the other. This ability to focus on the other person is the most important quality for ministers of care.

Your own quiet is a manifestation of such patience. It permits a wider range of responsiveness from the people you visit. Often full of self-concern, the sick person needs someone to listen. To listen effectively, the minister of care needs to be quiet.

Everyone loves to talk. It sets us at ease, allows us to make connections and permits us to do something. But ministers of care are called upon to encourage the other person to talk — and then to listen well. This is not easy.

Good Listening

One of the hardest aspects of good listening is putting out of our mind what we think the other will say. How do we listen with quiet patience? Here are three things that can help:

Attend. Physically pay attention. Look into the other person's eyes. Position your body so she or he can see you. Be interested. (Look interested, too!) What looks easy — giving attention — can be very hard work. Remember, there are many competing forces between you and the other, and within you as well. The other's reactions cause you to react. Any disabilities in speech, hearing, vision or mobility can make good communication a challenge. Add to that the environment of the hospital, nursing home or household, and you have much to distract you. Also, the listener can be distracted from within. Your own distress, your feelings for the other, your memories, even your upcoming grocery shopping can distract you. So work at being attentive. Focus on the other.

Notify. Let the person know that you hear what is being said. Nod occasionally. Lean forward to express your interest. One of the great

things about being in conversation with someone who pays attention to you is to see his or her physical reaction. The listener's eyes are warm (maybe they even sparkle); the listener leans forward so as not to miss a word; he or she even ignores the other sights and sounds all around. A good listener talks occasionally to let you know that he or she has understood, even adding his or her own ideas sometimes. Remind yourself to provide regular feedback when you listen. No matter how much you care inside, the person you visit won't know unless you notify on the outside.

Develop (and dig). Ask questions. As you hear something of interest, ask more specific questions. Allow more time for reflection. Psychiatrist Rudolf Dreikurs once said that in counseling, you will come upon "gold mines." These are precious parts of a conversation that can lead to deeper insights. Sometimes they are casual references: "Well, it's better than my *last* surgery." ("So you've had surgery before? What for?") "That nurse is *much* nicer than the one on duty at night." ("Are you having difficulty with the night nurse? What's happening?") "I don't want to *bore* you with the details of what she said that hurt so much." ("I'm not bored. Do you want to talk about it?") Each of these casual references is an opportunity for a minister of care to ask questions and talk more. Dreikurs said, "When you come upon a gold mine . . . dig!" Ask gentle questions.

Notifying and developing can be difficult habits to acquire. They are responses to what you hear and see. Such responses cannot be planned or rehearsed. The best listeners are spontaneous. The reason they succeed is not based on what they say, it is based on what they hear. The tools you are reviewing now can be useful in any situation. Ask any cabinetmakers how they produce such expert work and they will always give credit to their tools. Of course, it takes more than a good saw to fashion great furniture, but every artisan, every musician, every expert in anything is humbled by the power of a good tool in the right hands. A famous sculptor, about to begin work on a large piece of stone, once said, "My job is to find the statue that already exists within the rock and to bring it forth." So too with listening. Use your skills. Don't worry about a finished product. Focus on listening — now. Use the five R's.

The Five R's

The five R's of effective listening are listed in order of difficulty, with the easiest listed first:

Repeat. Say precisely what you heard the other person say. Repeat it back. This may feel awkward, but only to you. It won't feel awkward to the person with whom you are speaking. Use the exact words the person used.

Patient: I'm worried about my operation tomorrow.

Minister of care: You're worried about your operation tomorrow?

Patient: Yes, it's important, but there are so many unknowns.

Minister of care: Unknowns?

Patient: Well, we don't know . . .

Note that when you repeat, the other will continue with their line of thought. That's precisely what you want to happen. You want the person to talk about what he or she wants to talk about in the way he or she wants to talk about it. When you use this technique, add nothing to the conversation that is yours in the beginning. Repeating will help you listen. Don't use it exclusively, but start with it.

Restate. Here, repeat what was said, but use your own words. This will feel more comfortable for you, but it's possible that your meaning won't match the other person's meaning. If you find that your interpretation is not quite right, go back and repeat word for word, phrase by phrase, using the repeat technique.

Patient: I'm worried about my operation tomorrow.

Minister of care: Worried about the seriousness of the procedure?

Patient: Not really, it's just that tomorrow is my son's sixteenth birthday and I'd like to be with him.

Minister of care: Oh, you'd like to be there to celebrate with him.

Patient: Yes, I was hoping to hand him the keys myself.

Minister of care: Hand him the key? *(Repeat)*

Patient: Yes, to the car. He can drive now. I remember when my dad. . . .

Notice here the flow of the conversation as well as the use of the repeat technique when the minister of care wasn't sure what the patient meant. The focus for restating is the same as for repeating—the other is the focus.

Reflect. In addition to repeating or restating, the skill of reflecting allows you to act as a mirror for the feelings of the other person. Underneath much of what is said are the person's deeper feelings. The tone of what is said will reveal those feelings. Here the listener attempts gently to identify the feelings heard (sad, mad, angry, glad, happy, scared, hurt).

Patient: I just can't get over it.

Minister of care: Get over it? *(Repeat)*

Patient: That my roommate died. She was here yesterday, gone today.
    (Minister of care shows interested silence.)

Patient: It's just so, so crazy, so . . .

Minister of care: It's scary for you? *(Reflect)*

Patient: Very! Yes, very scary. That could be me, couldn't it?

Minister of care: I admire the way you can get in touch with your feelings. It's frightening when something like that happens close to you.

Patient: And we only knew each other for a couple of days.

Minister of care: I can tell she was important to you even though you knew each other just a short time. *(Restate)*

Patient: She was . . .

Here the feelings are of primary interest. There is no sympathy, pity or problem-solving: just a conversation between two people about an unchangeable life event. Feelings are in abundance. It is likely that no one else will attend to these feelings. Nurses, doctors, relatives and friends probably will not have an opportunity to hear about this patient's concern. Ministers of care can and do.

Respond. Sometimes words are not enough. Tears and laughter express what words can't. Touch helps us communicate beyond the words.

Silence allows for a deeper sense of understanding. A nod can give support. These responses signal your attentive listening and go beyond words.

Patient: It's just been so long . . .

   (Minister of care shows interested *silence*.)

Patient: So long since my husband's been gone. He was wonderful, you know.
   (Minister of care gives a slight *smile* and a *nod*.)

Patient: He knew me in ways no one else ever will, you know?

Minister of care: (nodding) I can tell you were very close.

Patient: Yes. You would have liked him.

Minister of care: (*touching* the hand of the patient, slightly) I imagine you're right!

The minister of care is relaxed and spontaneous, helping the other person relate memories.

Respect. Respect permeates good listening. Bernard Malamud once wrote, "Respect is what you have to have in order to get." Indeed, when we are respected by another person we feel respect for him or her. Respect as part of the listening process involves:

Understanding, not judgment
Caring, not criticism
Soft words, not harsh ones
Giving the benefit of the doubt
Enjoying the gifts of this person (however hidden they may be at the moment!)
Treating the person like a cherished friend or relative.

Patient: I just get so darn angry with those nurses.

Minister of care: Angry? *(Repeat)*

Patient: Yes, they make me wake up, poke at me, tell me this, tell me that.

Minister of care: It sounds like they boss you around a lot. *(Reflect)*

Patient: Worse. They think they know better. I'm a person. I don't have to be here.

Minister of care: It must be hard to take, an active person like yourself, having to be in here for a few days while you gain your strength back.

Patient: It is. I just want to go home.

   (Minister of care gives a slight *smile* and *nod.*)

Patient: It's not too much to ask for, is it?

Minister of care: I can tell you know what you want even if you don't get it right away.

Patient: Well, I know they have to do this and that. I just wish . . . I just wish . . .

Minister of care: Do you wish you could do it yourself?

Patient: Absolutely!

The minister of care is not engaging in fault-finding or even a detailed analysis of who did what to whom, but uses a respectful tone to help the person find out what she or he needs.

Giving Encouragement

Alfred Adler taught that mental health involves movement. When things are not going well, we say, "I'm stuck!" Our ability to keep going during good and bad times is a key to a healthy life. Encouragement helps us grow — helps us move. When we encourage another person, we are helping someone discover his or her heart. In fact, the root word in encouragement comes from the French *cœur:* heart. Illness and advanced age can sometimes be discouraging. Psychologist Michael Popkin recommends four ways to encourage others:

Show confidence in the person's ability to move through this situation. Showing confidence is more a way of being than a particular word or phrase. Remember you are seeing a person when their inner resources are at their utmost test. Don't try to diagnose — just work to understand.

Value the other person as she or he is. You won't like everyone you visit, and you don't have to. You just need to be with them on their journey. Value them as a fellow traveler, as a sign of Jesus with us.

Recognize the strengths of the other, even when those strengths are subtle or not obvious. Phrases such as: "I can tell . . ." "I'm aware . . ." and "May I tell you something that strikes me . . ." are affirmations that help others see their best selves through our eyes.

Stimulate independence and interdependence. It's easy to visit someone and to do things for them: help them eat, freshen their water and in other ways busy ourselves with tasks that help. But Rudolph Dreikurs cautions that we should never do anything for another that they could do for themselves. He wrote that it is disrespectful to do so — even with small children. When we stimulate independence, we are allowing others to feel their own power and self-control. This is not to say that we can't help. It is, though, a reminder that not all help is useful. Don't dote or pamper or do everything for those you visit. Even when it takes time, let them do what they can, when they want. We all want to be in control, even when we are debilitated by illness or age.

Know Yourself

Being aware of your own emotions is critical; your feelings will influence the quality of your visit and the effectiveness of your ministry. Asking yourself questions before and after each pastoral visit can be helpful:

Before the visit: How do I feel today? How do I feel about going on this visit today? Do I have any strong feelings about something else that might preoccupy me today?

After the visit: How do I feel now? What feelings have stayed with me? Which feelings do I need to reflect on? Which feelings do I need to talk about with someone else?

Emotions and feelings give us valuable information about ourselves only if we recognize them and accept them. Ministers of care may discover some emotions related to the ministry that they do not otherwise experience. You must exercise good judgment regarding these. Ask yourself: How do I feel? How will these feelings affect my visit? How can I move through these feelings to focus on the person I am visiting?

There are no absolute rules regarding emotions, but some guidelines may help. Psychiatrist Karen Horney has identified three ways that people move in relationship to one another: toward, away, against. Before making a pastoral visit, review your day and consider the times you have moved:

Toward – The times you have reached out, enjoyed or empowered someone.

Away – The times you have ignored, omitted or excluded someone.

Against – The times you have been angry, quarreled, or complained.

These ways of moving in a relationship underscore the choices we each have in our dealings with others. Applying these to the ministry of care, you will find that certain feelings will move you in one or more of these three directions with the person or the family you are visiting:

Toward – The "warm" emotions: happy, glad, enjoyable.

Away – The "cooler" emotions: afraid, disgusted, disappointed.

Against – The "hot" emotions: angry, jealous, hateful.

Depending on your experiences and your interpretations of those experiences, you respond in your unique way to different people that you visit and to the many things that are happening to them. When you sense some strong emotion, try to recall times when you had a similar experience. Your own past may help you gain an understanding of your present emotions.

It is less important to rid yourself of emotions that are troublesome to you than it is just to recognize them. The next time you are aware of an emotion that is giving you difficulty, don't simply force your way past it. Try to recognize it. Put a name on it, try to determine where it came from and then accept it. This will take you a long way in knowing about yourself and the person you are visiting.

One Final Skill

Perspective is a skill that anyone who works in healthcare needs in order to stay sane. Perspective allows us to visit a critically ill patient at 11:00 AM and then enjoy lunch with a friend at noon. Perspective allows us to cry with a cancer patient at 7:15 PM and delight in a new baby at 7:30 PM. Perspective allows us to empathize with the misfortunes of one family and celebrate the gift we have in our own.

Some hospital workers substitute distance for perspective. This is a mistake. You don't need to be remote to survive amid others' illnesses; you need to accept it as it is. There is good in the world as well as bad. There is health and disease. There is birth and death. In the ministry of care, you will see it all. As Jesus did.

Chapter 4

The Rites of the Sick

The church's ritual book, *Pastoral Care of the Sick*, provides rites for praying with sick adults or sick children, for giving communion to the sick, for giving communion to the dying (viaticum), for praying with the dying and for praying for the dead. All these services may be conducted by any member of the church, lay or ordained. The sacramental rites of anointing and penance are led by ordained priests, but other ministers may be asked to assist with the preparation and celebration of these rites.

Principles for Celebration

Several basic liturgical principles apply to the celebration of these rites, where circumstances allow. These principles aren't always convenient for the minister, but they contribute a great deal to the effectiveness of the celebration for those whom the minister serves. However, circumstances such as an emergency, a shared room or an intensive care unit may make it impossible to observe all of them.

Communal Celebration

Whenever possible, the rites are to be celebrated communally, that is, in a gathering of the faithful, however small. Invite family members, friends, other caregivers to participate as fully as they can. When it seems appropriate and feasible, ask someone other than the presiding minister to read, lead responses and state the intentions in the intercessory prayers. However, be careful not to add embarrassment to the other forms of stress suffered by the sick and those around them by placing them in roles in which they feel uncomfortable, without warning or without their consent.

Symbolic Richness

Ritual speaks more than one language. The rites can drown people in words, if their suffering makes it difficult for them to take in words. Brevity, imaginative language, song, even sung refrains, or one or two well-chosen visual symbols such as a Bible or a cross can break through the barriers of distraction raised by pain and carry the word of God into the hearts of those who hear. Silence is essential for words of power, and therefore, it, too, has its place in the celebration of the rites. The gestures of touch, such as a sign of the cross on the forehead, when performed with care and reverence, and the permission of the one to be touched, can bridge the sense of isolation brought about by sickness. But remember that sick people often feel resentful of the invasion of their person by relative strangers as required by medical care. Sensitive ministers will not presume that their touch is welcome. Ask permission.

Words of Power

All the dimensions of the rite must be allowed to speak with power. The word, for example, is best read from a Bible that is either made worthy by its beauty or holy by its long use as a family or personal bible. The entire rite, in fact, is best conducted from a book that bears silent witness to the dignity of the persons and the occasion, where so much that surrounds the sick is made of disposable paper and plastic. Water and the oil used by ordained ministers for anointing are to be visible and plentiful signs of the abundance of God's healing love. Everything that is used in the celebration must speak of God's care, expressed through the reverent care of the community, for those who suffer.

The Various Rites

Visits to the Sick

Chapters one and two of PCS offer an order for praying with sick adults and another for praying with sick children. Both follow a simple and familiar outline: reading(s), response, prayer — including the Lord's Prayer — and a final blessing. You will begin with an appropriate introduction or invitation to prayer. You may choose among various readings and prayers suitable for those present. On Sundays, the sick and those who are close to them may feel a closer bond with the parish community if they hear the readings used at Mass that day.

The order of prayer given for visits like this (which all Christians — not just the minister of care — can and should use frequently) are only suggestions. Sometimes you may want to add or substitute traditional prayers that bring comfort to the sick person: a Marian prayer or the "Glory be" doxology, for example. However, precedence should be given to prayers based on scripture in order to offer to the sick person and others present the comfort and the challenge of the word of God.

> VISITS TO THE SICK: OUTLINE OF THE RITE
> [Silent recollection]
> Reading
> Response
> The Lord's Prayer
> Concluding prayer
> Blessing

Communion for the Sick

Chapter three of PCS provides the rite of communion for use "in ordinary circumstances," and a shortened form for use "in a hospital or institution." The latter presupposes that one minister must give communion to a number of patients, perhaps within a limited amount of time.

The full communion service follows a familiar format: introductory rites (a greeting, an optional sprinkling with holy water and a short penitential rite); a liturgy of the word (one or more readings, a response, an optional period for silent reflection or short explanation of the word by the minister and general intercessions); the rite of holy communion (the Lord's Prayer, the giving of communion, a prayer after communion and a concluding blessing).

This order is familiar: It is similar to Mass, except, of course, that there is no eucharistic prayer. Familiarity is invaluable in time of stress; no one has to spend their energy on wondering what will come next. What changes from time to time is the choice of the readings and prayers and the reflections on the scripture by the minister. The language of the rite's

instruction makes it clear that any minister — lay or ordained — may give such an explanation.

The rite states that communion may be given under both kinds to all present who are eligible to receive it. It may not always be possible for each person to receive under both kinds: for example, a sick person may be unable to swallow the consecrated bread. In that case, every effort should be made to provide communion under the species of wine. The minister is directed to consume whatever remains after communion has been given. The parish staff will provide you with the necessary information and means for carrying the blood of Christ safely and for sharing it with someone who cannot sit up to receive it. It is always wise to make sure that a glass of water is on hand in case a sick person has trouble swallowing either the bread or the wine. You may break the bread further and give the person a smaller piece if necessary.

Although PCS offers a shortened form of the communion service for use in a hospital or an institution such as a nursing home, it discourages frequent use of this option. Rather than shortening the rite because of a shortage of ministers to serve many sick people, you are advised to consider gathering people together for a common celebration of the rite. The parish is also urged to appoint additional ministers. If neither is possible, add as much as possible from the full rite in each room with each person, especially the reading of the word. Remember, if the person you are visiting is very ill, or time is very short, a single sentence of scripture well chosen and even recited from memory is far better than no word at all. The distribution of communion must be accompanied by prayer. If at all possible, you should at least pray the Lord's Prayer with the communicant prior to giving communion.

> COMMUNION OF THE SICK: OUTLINE OF THE RITE
> [Silent recollection]
> Introductory Rites
> Greeting
> Sprinkling with holy water
> Penitential rite
> Liturgy of the Word
> Reading
> Response
> [Reading / acclamation / gospel]
> [Homily or reflection]
> General intercessions
> Liturgy of Holy Communion
> The Lord's Prayer
> Communion
> Silent prayer
> Prayer after communion
> Concluding Rite
> Blessing

Communion for the Dying: Viaticum

As those who are dying prepare to participate literally in the death and resurrection of Christ, sharing the eucharist is essential. The church uses formal language to express its urgency: "All baptized Christians who are able to receive communion are bound to receive viaticum by reason of the precept to receive communion when in danger of death from any cause." (PCS, 27) The word "viaticum" comes from the Latin, and means literally "the road, or way, or journey" (*via*) "with you" (*tecum*). The word expresses our firm belief that Jesus Christ is both the way through death to life everlasting and the companion who carries and sustains us on that last journey. We commonly translate the word as "food for the journey," or, as PCS translates it, "food for the passage through death to life." This food, of course, is the body and blood of Christ.

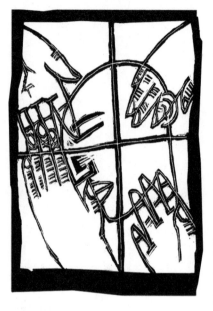

When death is relatively certain but slow in coming, every effort should be made to provide viaticum in the context of the Mass, even if the Mass is to be celebrated in the home of the dying person or in a hospital or another institution. The ideal is to give the person the opportunity to receive viaticum at a time when he or she can participate fully and consciously in the celebration, thus taking full advantage of the rich sustenance offered for this last phase of life's journey. When that is possible, the person may be able to receive communion again, perhaps even for several days. The minister of care should participate in the Mass and then may be called upon to bring communion in the days after, until the sick person dies.

The rite of viaticum outside of Mass follows the same pattern as an ordinary communion service, with some significant exceptions. During the penitential rite, a presiding priest may give the dying person what is called the "apostolic pardon" for the full remission of sin. The readings and prayers are especially chosen to speak honestly about the approach of death and of the life that awaits us beyond death. After the reading of the word and an optional brief explanation by the minister, the dying person is invited to renew the baptismal promises, which will be fulfilled in death. The communion rite may include a sign of peace in the usual place. PCS advises that "in this and in other parts of the celebration the sense of leave-taking need not be concealed or denied, but the joy of Christian hope, which is the comfort and strength of the one near death, should also be evident" (PCS, 100). Immediately after giving communion, the minister says to the dying person the words proper to the rite of viaticum: "May the Lord Jesus Christ protect you and lead you to eternal life." The entire ritual is a powerful sign that the Christian community is willing to allow its dying members the dignity of the truth, so often refused by a death-denying culture.

COMMUNION FOR THE DYING OUTSIDE OF MASS
OUTLINE OF THE RITE
[Silent recollection]
Introductory Rites
Greeting
Sprinkling with holy water
Instruction
Penitential rite
[Apostolic pardon]
Liturgy of the Word
Reading
Homily
Baptismal profession of faith
Litany
Liturgy of Holy Communion
The Lord's Prayer
Communion as viaticum
Silent prayer
Prayer after communion
Concluding Rite
Blessing
Sign of peace

Praying with the Dying

Particularly as hospice services become more available to care for the dying
and their loved ones, a minister may more frequently be called to the
bedsides of dying people with whom he or she has ministered throughout
the process of death. Ritual eases those moments when we are in the
presence of a mystery so great or an emotion so strong that words elude us.
Death is surely one of those occasions of power. PCS provides the minister,
and all Christians, with a rich array of prayers with which the community
can accompany the dying to the door of death and beyond it. There are no
rules for the use of these prayers, except the rule of reverence in the
presence of mystery.

The Prayers of Commendation are intended to be used while the person is still alive, but when death seems imminent. They include short lines from scripture, readings from scriptures, the litany of the saints, another litany for deliverance and prayers composed especially for the situation.

The Prayers after Death are for use immediately upon death. They not only invoke the saints and angels to accompany the soul of the dead Christian to God, but they also express the fear and sorrow (in Psalm 130) as well as the faith and trust (in Psalm 23) of the survivors.

These prayers can be found in PCS, chapter six, or in Liturgy Training Publications' small prayerbook, *Prayers with the Dying*. (See the front of this book for ordering information.)

Chapter 5

Being a Leader of Prayer

Many potential ministers of care are nervous about praying with the sick and leading the communion rite. They are especially fearful of having to improvise. *Pastoral Care of the Sick* supplies orders of prayer and the communion rite with many options to fit different needs and occasions. However, ministers may still be afraid that they won't do it right. Here are some simple principles that can help. For veteran ministers, or for those who already have experience in leading prayer in other circumstances, these principles can serve as a reminder of what has been learned by experience.

Be Prepared

Become familiar with the rites provided by PCS. Know what is in the book and where to find it. Even more important, perhaps, pray with the prayer texts and readings from time to time at home, so that you become a living word yourself, rather than a reader of words on a page. That is easier to do if you know the book so well that you can give your attention to the people present and to God rather than having to concentrate on the printed page.

Plan ahead as much as you can. PCS emphasizes that the sick and their families or friends should be encouraged to take part in planning and preparing the celebration. Often, sick people are reduced to merely passive receivers of treatments that are beyond their understanding or control; it is an expression of respect to invite them to take an active part in the rites and prayers. This is especially possible when a minister visits the same person regularly; the best way of celebrating the communion rite can be discerned over the first few visits and then repeated. For example, the sick person may regularly want to choose the reading, or if the Sunday scriptures are used, to proclaim the reading.

Before you go, make a list of what you will need during your visit. Decide what you might ask family members, friends or caregivers to have on hand, if circumstances permit, and what you might need to supply yourself. For example, you will need your ritual book. You might want to use a separate Bible or lectionary for the readings. If you will be giving communion, you'll need the eucharistic bread in a pyx (the container used to transport the eucharistic bread), and the eucharistic wine in a vial. A cross or other sacred image of Christ might be placed in some central spot to provide a focus of attention and to remind all those gathered that God is present and active in their midst, even in the most sterile of sickrooms. The environment for a communion service should include a cloth-covered table on which to set the eucharist. Candles may be used (see PCS, 74) at home and in some nursing homes, but not when oxygen is in use, for safety's sake.

When you arrive, after you have had a chance to talk with the sick person and the others present, spend a few minutes readying the room for prayer or communion. Make sure, for example, that you will have a convenient place to set your book while you distribute communion, or that a glass of water is available for a sick person who can't swallow easily. It is wise to choose with care the place where you stand and sit so that you can easily be seen and heard by all present. It is never appropriate to invade the sick person's space, sometimes that person's only privacy, by sitting on the bed or by using it as a shelf. Moreover, it is discourteous to force the sick person to lie or sit at an uncomfortable angle to see you.

Be Hospitable

Genuine hospitality includes making everyone feel welcome and putting them at their ease. You can make those present more comfortable by letting them know what to expect, especially if some of them are unfamiliar with Catholic worship. You need not give them a detailed, technical preview. However, if you have not visited this group of people before, you can give them a very brief outline. At a communion service, for example, you might say, "First, we'll take a moment of silence. After we've listened to a reading from scriptures, we'll have some time for quiet prayer and for intercessions before we share communion."

Make sure that those present know what they are expected to do. Arrange for someone to do the reading ahead of time. Many people are unaware that family, friends and other caregivers present may receive communion with the sick person, according to the usual norms for communion. (See PCS, 72.) You may want to mention that before beginning.

Make a clear beginning and a clear ending to the rite itself. The order of events during the visit will vary according to the needs of the one you are visiting. In some instances, the visit may begin as a social one, move into the ritual and then continue as a pastoral visit. In other cases, the pastoral visit will come first, the rite will follow and socializing may not be done at all. Sometimes the visit may be brief and concentrated on the rite itself. But never just dispense communion and run.

Social conversation, pastoral conversation and prayer require different styles of behavior. People are ill-at-ease if they're not sure whether to continue in an informal conversational mode or to adopt the more formal atmosphere that tends to mark ritual worship. Ministers who are reluctant to claim the role of leader of prayer sometimes mistake a chatty, humorous informality for authentic person-centered worship. Sickness and death are among life's ultimate mysteries. In the presence of these mysteries, we have a duty to show reverence if we believe, as we claim to, in the dignity of the sick and the dying. The time of prayer may be the only time when those present dare to drop the masks of cheerfulness with which they support each other and to share their pain truthfully before God. The minister can help a great deal by saying, at the appropriate moment, "Now let us spend a few moments in silence, preparing our hearts to pray and to hear the word of God." Then, after an honest pause, "In the name of the Father and the Son and the Holy Spirit." Similarly, after the blessing and dismissal at the end of the rite, the minister can say something like, "Now let us end our prayer in peace," and wait a moment before beginning to clear things away so that the people can readjust to a conversational mode.

Be Attentive

Listen. Even before prayer begins, listen to what the sick person and others present tell you with their words, with their eyes, with their facial expressions. (See chapter 3 to refresh your memory about the difference between a social visit and a pastoral one.) It's important to remember that what might seem to you a short reading, a short prayer, a short rite, can overtax the limited strength and patience of sick people or weary caregivers. You can make that judgment on the basis of what you hear from them. You will find many options among the prayers and readings of the rites. Attentive listening before you begin will allow you to choose what best fits the needs of the participants. (See PCS, 45, 47, 72.)

Listen to what is read and said, by yourself and by others, during the service itself. You may find that you hear the word of God with new ears as you see it mirrored on the faces of those around you. You may surprise yourself with the insights you are able to share, either formally during the service or in less formal conversation afterward, as a result of what you have heard.

Participate in Prayer

Pray while you lead. The word "minister" in Latin means "servant." You are a servant of the Lord present and acting in the word and the prayers and the people gathered. You will find, as you minister to the sick, that you yourself may be in need of God's healing touch as you confront the suffering of others. You need your prayer. Those gathered need your prayer to help them to pray. Prayer requires attention, time, care. It requires honesty and sincerity. It requires silence here and there. You might think of the frustrated woman who snapped, when a heedless minister rushed from "Let us pray," into the prayer text without drawing a breath, "Give me a minute! I'm trying, I'm trying!"

Chapter 6

Sharing the Word of God

The word of God is a word of power. In the first creation account in the book of Genesis, God draws an ordered universe and life out of chaos by means of the word. In the gospel of John, God draws life in its fullness out of the chaos of sin and death that still swirled through unredeemed creation by means of the word made flesh, Jesus Christ. And Jesus raised Lazarus to life out of the chaos of death by means of a word.

It makes great good sense, then, at times of sickness and death, to confront the chaos they bring into the lives of sufferers with the power of the word of God. *Pastoral Care of the Sick* emphasizes the value of reading and praying from scripture with and for the sick and the dying. (See PCS, 65.)

PCS provides an extensive set of readings for use in praying with the sick and the dying, in giving communion and viaticum and in celebrating the sacrament of the anointing of the sick. (See PCS, 297.) There are nine readings taken from the books of Kings, Job, Wisdom and the prophet Isaiah. One of the readings from Job is recommended for use with the dying. There are 23 readings taken from the book of Acts, the letters of Paul to the Romans, Corinthians, Galatians, Philippians and Colossians, the letter to the Hebrews, the letters of James, Peter and John and the book of Revelation. Four of them are recommended for use with the dying. There are 14 psalm selections for use as responsorial psalms and several verses for use as gospel acclamations. There are 20 gospel passages; two of them are recommended for use with the dying. In addition, there is a special set of readings for use in the celebration of eucharist with viaticum. (See PCS, 298.)

How to Choose Readings

How is a minister to choose? The essential criterion, repeated again and again in PCS, is the need of the hearers. Awareness of their physical condition will determine how many readings are to be used in a particular service and how long those readings can be. Concern for their spiritual needs will determine which readings are chosen. Sometimes a minister may not know precisely what those needs are, but can discern them from the general tenor of the conversations that have taken place. At other times, the minister must simply rely on God to speak through whatever is selected. The results can be surprising.

When making regular visits each Sunday to bring communion, the minister of care may want to use the Sunday lectionary readings to help the homebound person hear the word of God that the whole church is hearing.

Know the Choices

The minister who has become familiar with the lectionary through personal prayer and reflection on the experiences of praying with the sick and dying might want to consider the following questions when choosing the readings.

With which character or point of view expressed in the passage are the hearers most likely to identify? A sick person who feels discouraged, for example, might easily identify with the prophet Elijah in 1 Kings 19:4 – 8, PCS, 297. (Unfortunately, the selection omits the earlier verses in which the reason for Elijah's discouragement is apparent: He is out of a job because of the queen's displeasure. For sick people who are discouraged because they are unable to work or have lost their jobs, the minister might want to add those verses or explain the situation after the reading.)

Someone who is angry with God or with suffering might be gratified to hear those feelings powerfully and bitterly expressed in three passages from the book of Job: 3:3, 11 – 17, 20 – 23; 7:1 – 4, 6 – 11; or 7:12 – 21. Family members grieving over the illness or approaching death of a loved one might hear Jesus speak of their mourning in the beatitudes from Matthew 5:1 – 12. Caregivers might see themselves in those praised for visiting Christ in the sick in Matthew 25:31 – 40. (All of these passages are in PCS, 297.)

Know the Hearers

Is the identification likely to help the hearers? Angry people who hear their feelings spoken by Job might find great relief from guilt about their anger with God when they realize that their anger is given voice in the very word of God itself. The grieving might take heart at hearing themselves called "blessed" and reminded that joy follows grief. Weary sufferers might find comfort in Jesus' invitation and promise to all those who labor and are burdened in Matthew 11:25–30 (PCS, 297, Gospel D). However, a blind person who identifies with blind Bartimaeus but is not, like Bartimaeus, cured (see Mark 10:46–52, PCS, 297, Gospel I), might begin to question either the adequacy of his or her personal faith or the arbitrariness of God in curing some but not others. Similarly, someone who is struggling with faith might feel desperately guilty upon hearing Jesus' rebuke to the disciples for their lack of faith after he stills the storm (Mark 4:35–41, PCS, 297, Gospel H).

Many of the stories in which Jesus is shown healing the sick or raising the dead are not in fact as comforting as they might seem to people who have no reasonable hope of recovery. People who are sick and those who love them sometimes grasp at any straw that might carry them out of the flood of their suffering. Apparent promises of cure for those whose faith is strong can cause untold harm when the promises are not kept for these listeners. If a reading might cause unnecessary pain or confusion because of the kind of identification it invites, either choose another reading or offer a word of explanation that will prevent misinterpretation of the message.

What kind of conversion of heart does the reading invite? The reign of God requires of us all constant growth. Many of the readings address the demand for deeper faith, greater hope and unselfish love that is implicit in an experience of sickness. The New Testament readings are especially forceful in strengthening these qualities by direct exhortation. They often may be successfully combined with an Old Testament or gospel passage in such a way as to make explicit the call to conversion expressed through story in those selections. Sometimes you can offer a similar growth in insight by an imaginative choice of an Old Testament passage and a gospel selection that strike sparks from one another in the listeners' imagination. For example, the prophet Elijah is provided with bread that strengthens him to make the journey to Mount Horeb, where he will have a powerful encounter with God, as a minister who has read further might point out. This passage can make one of the familiar selections from the bread of life discourse in John 6:51 and 6:54 – 58, in PCS, 84 and 297, come to life for the weary and discouraged hearer who will receive communion.

Choose Carefully

There is more in this lectionary than meets the eye — or the ear — on first reading it. Only a hurried and harried minister will settle for the comforting stories of Jesus curing the sick. Sometimes those stories are appropriate; sometimes they are not. Often there is much fruit to be had by preparing with a prayerful reading of the passages, or perhaps a combination of passages, while asking these questions: Why was this passage included in this lectionary? To whom might it be addressed? What might it say in these particular circumstances? Such questions invite us to hear familiar words with new ears in the particular context of sickness and suffering.

God is astonishingly creative. The word of God can find the most amazing ways to slip through the cracks of the barriers of familiarity, boredom or resistance that we can raise against the possibility of being touched by the liturgy of the word. The minister serves an imaginative and compassionate savior, whose every word gives life, even in the presence of illness and death.

Chapter 7

Organizing the Visit

The circumstances of visiting someone at home are different from those surrounding a visit to a hospital, hospice or other facility, but the general ideas presented here are adaptable for any kind of pastoral visit. When visiting someone at home, for example, always call ahead and make an appointment. You cannot do that for hospital visits (see pages 44 – 48), but you can, and should, knock on the door and ask if it's a good time to visit.

Before the Visit

Make an appointment. Even if you have a regularly scheduled time for visiting (after Mass every Sunday, for example), call to confirm since the situation can change: The person may not be up for a visit, relatives may have decided to come over and the like.

Don't visit if you are sick. The common cold may be seriously dangerous for a person who is already ill. Call to cancel your appointment if you are not well.

Spend time in prayer. If you're going to be bringing communion, perhaps you can spend time praying in the blessed sacrament chapel at church.

Check your emotions. Use the questions on page 21.

Gather what you need. Did you promise to bring something? Find your ritual book, pyx and other needed items.

The ride over. This is your final opportunity to settle yourself. Turn off the radio and reflect. Pray some more. (But don't let this be the only time that you pray!) Sort out your day and let it take a back seat to your visit.

During the Visit

Be friendly. Be cheerful, open and warm. It is better to be moderately friendly at first: Be cautious about being seen as too friendly or overpowering. On the other hand, be careful not to let any natural shyness make you appear remote or distant. Start with a smile.

Be flexible. Every visit is different. Be prepared for nothing to be routine. Interruptions may happen. You will be a better visitor if you can go with the flow.

Be alert. Be aware of the events, the people and the environment. Let part of yourself be an observer. Then if it is appropriate, you can use that observation in your ministry. For example, if you are visiting and the grandchildren — who were crying, playing and into everything — have just left, you might say, "Well, you certainly have an active group there!" or, "I admire your ability to make your grandchildren feel so welcome here," or, "Tell me about your grandchildren!" No grandparent alive will pass up that chance.

Be confident. No one is an expert all the time. Even the best ministers of care are not always as confident as they would like to be. But an air of confidence will help tremendously. Even if you don't feel confident, quietly act as if you do. It will help you and the person you visit. This is called the "as if" principle in modern psychology: Though we don't always feel something, we can act "as if" we do. And many times when we act "as if," we wind up feeling that we actually do!

Be personal. Feel free to ask questions, speak of feelings, listen intently, nod and respect what is being told to you. It is the other person's needs that are primary, not your own. That doesn't mean that every visit delves into deep or intimate matters. Some people will want and need nothing more than a pleasant visit.

Be yourself. You'll be at your best when you can be yourself within the context of your ministerial role of being a person of prayerful presence. Even though we all need certain communication skills for this ministry, the interesting part of the ministry of care is that you really can be yourself with this service. Yes, some of us are a bit too timid at times, some too loud, some too careful and the like. Psychologist Frank Walton says that the point isn't perfection, it's about reaching out to another in need, and lovingly, however imperfectly, communicating to them that we are there with them — being prayerful presence with a purpose.

Ending the Visit

End with appropriate verbal encouragement. Say something like, "Thank you for letting me visit with you today. Please keep me in your prayers. I'll keep you in mine." This can be a very encouraging statement, since it helps the person offer service back to you through prayer. It might be helpful to connect the verbal encouragement with nonverbal communication, for example, making the sign of the cross on the person's forehead (one more time, if you concluded a rite that way), a handshake or a smile of encouragement.

One-Time Visits

Sometimes you will be called upon to visit a person just once. A person may be in the hospital for routine tests or the person is to be discharged soon. It may be helpful to say things like, "If the parish can be any help, this is my phone number. Please call," or, "This is the phone number of the parish office; they can get in touch with me." Do not say something like, "I'll see you next time I come," because many times people take that literally. They may think that you are promising to see them again and that is not the case.

Long-Term Visits

Many ministers of care prefer these visits because they can develop a rapport with the person. They come to know what to expect and they can develop a friendship. Some ministers, however, are not able to commit the time or the energy to something that could last a long time.

Be sure that the visits continue to be pastoral; don't let them become simply social visits. That's a fine line, especially hard when you develop a friendship. Do a lot of reflecting on the visits, alone and sometimes with your parish coordinator.

Sporadic Visits

Because of the nature of a person's illness or hospitalization, you may see a person once, then a couple of times a few months later and then perhaps not again for a year. These intermittent, unpredictable visits create a relationship, but also a frustration. Try to link the visits together in conversation remembered from the last time. "How have you been? What's been going on since we met a few months ago?" Help the person reflect on the changes that have happened.

Sometimes these visits occur with cancer patients who go into the hospital for periodic treatments. Such people see you when they are involved with this special kind of pain in their lives. It is all right if you don't remember details about the person and have to ask again, but when asking, acknowledge having met before. For example: "You know, I've forgotten your children's names. Could you tell me again?" Such a question shows a continuity — and also shows that you are human. If you forget quickly, you will find it helpful to make notes after a visit and to keep a simple file to which you can refer if you visit again weeks later.

After the Visit

Ministers of care have found these suggestions to be useful in working through the visit after it is over.

Write in a journal. Many ministers of care write about their visits in a confidential journal just for themselves. Don't use people's names, but name your own experiences and feelings. The purpose is not to diagnose the person you visited, but to help you process your own thoughts and feelings.

Reconnect with your community. Join other ministers of care on a regular basis and talk through your own experiences. Ministers of care need to be ministered to!

Debrief. Especially after a tougher visit, call another minister of care or your parish coordinator and talk it over soon after the visit. Not all visits will go smoothly. Part of our job is to learn from each visit. This debriefing process helps. It also has another advantage: It's more practice using our skills. Use all your skills as much as possible, even with another minister of care. You'll get better and more natural with each practice.

Follow up. Did you promise to do something for the person you visited? Do you need to inform the pastor of a change in the person's condition? Follow up when necessary.

Make notes. When you are likely to make many visits to the same person, it can be helpful to keep a card with the person's name, interests dates of visits, and the like, to stimulate your memory. If an index card can help you recall something of particular interest (a special anniversary, a good experience with a grandchild and other things of that nature), then you can be that much more comfortable in showing active interest in the person you are visiting.

Take quiet time. Reflect on what you have gained from this visit. Ministry of care is a mutual ministry — sometimes we gain more than we give. Ask yourself the questions on page 21.

Prepare for the next visit. While it is not possible to predict the future, reflecting on what you just experienced can help you be ready for the next time. You may want to make notes for yourself.

Spend time with family and friends. Take time to enjoy your own family and friends. And remember, you don't have to be a minister of care to them! The people you visit in your role as a minister of care will benefit from your involvement with your own family and friends. The healthier you are, the healthier your ministry will be.

Chapter 8

Visiting in Hospital
and Nursing Home

Visiting people who are in the hospital or in a nursing home can be quite a different experience from visiting someone who is homebound. The environment is totally different, and whereas you may repeatedly visit a homebound person, you may see a person in the hospital only once or twice. You may visit a person in a nursing home regularly, but the conditions are quite different than visiting a person at home. This chapter discusses the unique and challenging circumstances of making pastoral visits to people in a hospital or nursing home.

The Initial Visit

At the beginning of a hospital or nursing home visit, introduce yourself clearly and distinctly: "My name is Pat Smith. I'm a minister of care from St. Mary's Church on Main Street. The pastor, Father Ken Brown, asked me to stop in and see you."

This tells the person who you are, where you are from and indicates someone the sick person might know on the parish staff. Your opening line does not have to be well rehearsed, but it needs to be genuine.

Next, relate to the situation:

"How are you doing?"
"How are things going here?"
"How can I be of help?"

These are all appropriate questions to open a conversation. This is where you use all your skills of listening and understanding and of sharing yourself and representing your community. Try to be as natural as you can. Your goal at this point is to establish a relationship.

Remember to use the 5 R's from pages 17– 20. Resist the natural temptation to feel inadequate in this work. Resist the discouraging thought that you may not be doing it right. Resist the fear of making a mistake. All of these feelings are natural, but they are not useful.

Instead, remind yourself that you are here because of a call to ministry. You are not here because you are perfect. You are here because you are human. Remember that you are not alone. You represent a faith community and a world-wide church that is praying for this visit. Remember that Christ is present.

The visit may come to a close because of your schedule, because visiting hours are almost over or because a doctor or other visitors have arrived. It is appropriate, but optional, to talk about another visit. If you can make another visit, say something like, "Would it be all right if I came back tomorrow?" You may also ask, "Will it be all right with you if another minister of care visits you in the near future?" Do not talk about coming back unless you are absolutely certain that you can. Then it is time to say good-bye and go. As you leave, ask yourself, "What should I do as a result of this visit?"

General Guidelines

1. Stop at the nurses' station. Check with the staff. Tell them who you are, why you are there and ask if this is the proper time to visit. Sometimes the nurses will advise you of recent medication, pain or sleep patterns.

2. If the door to the patient's room is closed, ask the nurse if it is all right to enter. Be careful to observe "No visiting" or "Isolation" signs hanging on the door. If the light over the patient's door is lit, do not enter until the nurse has taken care of the patient's needs and has told you that your visit is permissible. Then knock and enter upon invitation to do so.

3. Always let the patient take the lead in shaking hands. Do not touch, lean or sit on the patient's bed. Even a slight movement can increase pain. Upon entering the room stand or sit in line with the patient's vision, so that the patient is not required to move around to see you.

4. Beware of letting the visit become a medical conference. Don't make a habit of sharing your own hospital experience or that of another with the patient. The patient is the teacher, you are the student.

5. Help the patient to relax by being relaxed yourself. Do not carry emotional "germs" from one room to another. Rest between room visits if you need to.

6. Do not whisper or speak in low tones to a nurse, to a member of the family or to anyone else in or near the room.

7. You might leave when the patient's meal is delivered. Ask — the patient will let you know.

8. Speak to every patient present. Roommates are people too.

9. Do not make the visits too long. End on a positive note.

Difficulties

A minister of care may confront some difficulties, such as the examples here.

1. Many times the patient in a hospital or a nursing home is under severe anxiety and stress. This may not be obvious. An experienced minister of care learns to read the signals carefully. If you sense that the patient's spirit is low, allow him or her to express the full range of emotions. Permit a wide range of conversation if this seems to be helping.

2. Sometimes the patient has visitors when you arrive. Your visit can happen when others are present, but more often you may wish to say, "I see you have friends here now. Would it be all right if I came back later today or tomorrow afternoon?" With a terminally ill patient, some members of the family may always be there. Your visit is as much for the family members as it is for the person that you originally came to see.

3. The television, present in nearly every hospital room, can be a problem. Television is a great distraction. Frequently, the patient cannot turn it off because the other patient in the room is watching. You may offer to come back when the program has ended. The patient may then accept your offer or suggest that you stay. If the latter happens, you can simply ask, "Would you like me to turn the TV off for a little while?"

4. The hospital staff performs procedures all during the day. Your visit may be interrupted by doctors, nurses or even volunteers from the hospital. If it seems appropriate, offer to wait in the hall. Excuse yourself by saying aloud, "I'll step out for a few minutes, Mrs. Verdi. I'll be back when the doctor is finished. Is that all right with you?"

The relationship that you develop with the patient — even if you make only two or three visits — is very important to the patient. You will be surprised how long your visits will be remembered — by them and by you! We can never plan for all situations, but we can be ready for them. Televisions, doctors, visitors, patients who are sleeping or recovering from medication all go with the territory for the minister of care who visits people in hospitals or nursing homes. You'll get better at handling them as your experience with this ministry increases.

Nursing Homes

Nursing homes require a special commitment. They often demand longer-term, more predictable visits. Some of the visits require more patience and some visits may require a kind of advocacy — you may be the one to keep the nurse and the professional staff, even the administration, in touch with the person's needs and treatment. Nursing home visits require a special stamina. Not everyone is good at this. If this is not your particular talent, offer to visit those at home or in the hospital instead.

Residents in nursing homes have had to adjust to a very different way of life. Living in a nursing home is a very public experience. Everyone sees everyone daily. Many residents don't know when — or if — they can go home. They are being encouraged to be more independent and to accept the routine care of the staff at the same time.

Many of the residents have lost their mobility, sight, financial control, their homes — in a word, they have lost their independence. Elderly nursing home residents are watching their former lives disappear. Younger residents may be the victims of stroke, disease or accidents, and are living in a limited world where they are in the minority. Their social contacts can be very strained.

Some residents are undergoing regular therapy to re-learn the most basic of skills. These residents are learning to feed themselves, to walk, to dress, play bingo, watch TV — and for some, it is excruciatingly hard to do these simple things. Some residents are unable to feed themselves, and are unable to communicate as well. During the hustle and bustle of meal times, nursing homes frequently deploy staff members who might be called "tray runners"— their assignment is to pick up the food trays after meals. Sometimes busy workers remove a tray although it has not been touched. Be aware of this and other situations like this, and report them to the nursing home administration.

Some residents appear unresponsive, as if they do not understand what is going on around them, but you need to be aware that they may very well understand perfectly. Don't be deceived by outward appearances. What the inner mind knows, we may not always be able to show. Respect people in this situation. Never say anything around them that you wouldn't want them to hear if they were their former selves.

During a visit, never move a patient yourself. Ring for the staff. That's their job, and they know how to do it with a minimum of risk to the patient—or to themselves.

Don't disappoint the nursing home resident by not showing up when you promised. Your visit may be the most important part of their week. You don't have to visit every day, just regularly and predictably. It is permissible to limit your visits: "I can stay for half an hour today. Would you like me to ask someone to push your wheelchair into the garden so we can visit there, or would you like to stay inside?" Watch for signs of fatigue. Don't overstay or overtalk your welcome.

Loneliness is a chronic disease in nursing homes. At least in a hospital, so much is happening that there is an immediate hope of going home. The nursing home may be the last home that some residents will have. Visitors all eventually leave. Residents often don't.

The quality of professional care in nursing homes varies greatly. Watch for signs of abuse or neglect, and tell your parish coordinator or pastor if you are alarmed. Help the families of the residents be vigilant. If you are afraid something is wrong, tactfully bring it up.

Chapter 9

Concerns and Pitfalls

Yogi Berra once said, "We made too many wrong mistakes." Here are some common situations and potential difficulties, so you won't make too many wrong mistakes.

Dealing with Differences

Here are some guidelines to help you recognize the different kinds of people you may minister to.

Some people are most comfortable with one-to-one relationships. They are friendly, they smile, they complain little, they seem to be more interested in you than in having you be interested in them. They enjoy give-and-take conversation, and may not talk about themselves very much. You can be informal with people like this and allow for a slower pace. They appreciate eye contact, family talk and warmth. They especially like to be liked. Author Tony Alessandra has called people who face the world this way "relators" because they like one-to-one relationships.

Others, who are more comfortable with groups of people, tend to be more spontaneous, lively and even fun to be with. These are the people who have a bit of sparkle in their personality and in their eyes. Their conversation flows. Even if they are in pain, they strive to use humor and light talk. There's a good bit of the entertainer in them. They like to be enjoyed and they are usually full of stories. People like this are called "socializers" because they like the social scene and many different kinds of relationships happening simultaneously.

Another type is more analytical, cognitive and precise. These people tend to be more serious, conservative and quiet. They are not always very sociable, but they are willing to talk about subjects they know well. They appreciate conversations where they can be the teacher. Discussing

feelings may not be comfortable, so expect some silences. They may be a bit more introverted: Allow for longer warm-up times. Second visits usually go better with these people than first visits. People who like to think about things before they talk or act are called "thinkers."

Some people are very direct, assertive and task-oriented. People like this may appear rough, especially when they are in pain or under pressure. They can be forceful and very directive. They usually say what they mean and mean what they say. Let them control the conversation. Don't expect them to talk much about feelings. They are comfortable with anger and they usually don't mean to put you off by it. People who like to be in charge are called "directors."

(For more information on these four types of personalities, see the book *People Smart* by Tony Alessandra. Call 1-800-222-4383 for more information.)

Understanding Different People

People react to fear and suffering in different ways, sometimes quite harshly. Don't be put off. Each person is doing his or her best to cope. The minister of care can bring a prayerful presence to each of these sufferers.

When you hear someone issuing commands, it is likely that he or she wants to take control. It's a possibility that the person feels powerless at that time. Many people have a hard time being hospitalized: patients have very, very little control. So listen to them. Don't be intimidated. Reflect their feelings using the 5 R's. If they are particularly difficult, try to remember the last time you felt out of control. That may help you appreciate their fear.

Know-it-alls also want to be in control but they do it by feeling that they are correct. A psychologist once said that the greatest feeling in life can be the feeling of being right. It's hard to feel right when, as a patient, other people know what is best for you. People like this may be sticklers for detail and precision. They may even correct you! You may feel that they hold a superior attitude. Others feel this about them also. They like to relate their accomplishments and their experiences. So ask questions.

When you hear someone interrogating, it's likely that this person needs to find solutions and wants to know who is responsible. People who do this find not knowing to be very difficult — it drives them crazy! And they can drive everyone else crazy as they try to get to the bottom of things. Hospitals are full of people to interrogate, so interrogators have plenty of people to talk to. Answer their questions, but don't get too caught up in your story. Finish your answer by turning the question back to the interrogator with a phrase like "And you?" Try to get them to talk about half the time, although this may not be easy.

People who suffer in silence are frequently trying to protect someone else from being hurt. The silent sufferer pushes his or her own feelings down so that others (perhaps family members) won't worry. It might be worthwhile to try to get him or her to open up to you.

Someone who uses sarcasm or plays psychologist frequently wants to escape from a feeling of inferiority. One way people try to do this is to denigrate someone else, even subtly. So he or she will speak about hidden meanings and motivations and may be very suspicious. Don't be deterred from conversation. Keep it simple and directed to this person.

Those who are angry with God and everyone else are desperately trying to find a way out of the darkness they feel. Their brooding and bad moods are an attempt to make sense of a very confusing situation. People like this need you to be on the journey with them. Don't lead, don't follow, just be with them, as you would with a good friend.

Families

Each person in the patient's family has his or her own reaction to the disease or disability. At times, there may be a need for the minister of care to visit the spouse, parent or other member of the family. A cup of coffee in the hospital cafeteria or a chat while walking down the hallway can be good for all concerned. Research with families of cancer victims shows that the family suffers also. Respond to the individuals within the family and not just to the family as a unit.

Not all families cope with illness gracefully. For busy families, illness is a real inconvenience and causes tremendous fear. You may even hear anger in their voices, for they are indeed angry! You may be the safest person for them to talk with.

Illness puts many pressures on the family, psychologically, spiritually, financially and physically. We might think that these concerns pale in comparison to the actual illness, but this is not always the case. Every member of every family is different. Family life goes on. Sports, school, childcare, work — all must go on. You will hear lots of talk about this. Just listen. Each family will figure out how to do these important jobs. When they talk about them, they're also expressing their deeper feelings.

Each child will respond in his or her own way. Pay special attention to the quiet ones who seem to be coping just fine. Quiet children need a prayerful person to talk with as much as their more clearly needy siblings do.

Adolescents need the right time, the right place, the right words, with the right person — and the right person may be you. Be alert to signs that the adolescent wants to talk with you. Teens will wait to see if you can be trusted before making a move. When they talk, be a trustworthy friend.

Take nothing personally. If you do, you may lose your ability to function as a minister of care with a particular family. Think of being a sailboat during a storm. You can't control the wind, only your own sails.

If it is appropriate, you may wish to arrange for tangible help from your parish. Food, babysitters, funeral arrangements, school tuition or other assistance may be available for the family from your parish. Get permission from the family first, and then make the necessary calls, but don't provide any of this assistance yourself. Be steadfast in your role as a minister of care. If you become the babysitter, the cook or the provider of money, you confuse the family about your role of prayerful presence. You are a minister of care first, last and always.

Appreciate each family. Look for the positive differences and the uniqueness. This will encourage the family, and help you to serve them well during this most stressful time.

Stress

The ministry of care is not easy. It takes a toll on many of us even if we are well prepared for it. Your attitude is an important part of this ministry; be confident of what you are supposed to do and of what you are not supposed to do, of what you can do and what you cannot do. A minister can easily become over-involved and over-extended.

You cannot take on all the cares of every family that you visit. Here are some suggestions for dealing with stress:

Be aware. Stay alert for signs of fatigue and irritability in yourself. If you feel nervous and anxious, recognize it, name it and feel it. Emotions will be expressed one way or another. It's better to acknowledge them than to ignore them.

Know yourself. Know your limits. Acknowledge and take into account your own experience. If you are aware that you are not having a good day, remember that that is human and normal.

Trust your emotions. If you feel angry, sad, happy, scared or hurt, allow yourself to feel that way. Knowing what you feel is initially more important than addressing your feelings.

Consider your alternatives. What are your choices? What can you do? Some time alone, a walk around the block or some time in the chapel may help you discern the possibilities.

Do something. Doing something, especially something physical, will give you the feeling of being more in control. More importantly, even if your action is nothing dramatic, it will give you more options.

Reflect. How did things work out? Do a quick "before and after" checklist in your head. This will allow for a faster process next time you're under stress. You'll discover more about yourself as well.

Silences

Silences sometimes happen because people are reflecting and sometimes because people don't know what to say. Silence can feel awkward for the minister of care. Sometimes you may feel your job is to make the conversation flow. You may feel pressure to make the visit a good one by chatting. Remember that silence probably indicates that the person is resting or thinking. People need this silence. One way to become more comfortable with needed silence is this: When you have said something and there is a silence, allow a full sixty seconds by your watch to pass before you say anything more. This will force you to allow silence. You'll see that it is not a catastrophe.

One of the gifts we human beings have is our ability to make choices. We decide what we say and do, when we talk and act, and often what we feel. Choose to take your time. Let moments of silence into your conversations. Silences can be grace moments, when we can be aware of God's presence.

Rejection

It is the right of patients to see only the people they want to see. One day a patient may not want you around. A patient may reject you as a minister of care. Accept that. Don't challenge it. Rejection by a patient is almost never personal. It has nothing to do with who you are or with what kinds of skills you have used.

Act professionally. None of us likes to be rejected. Eventually a patient will reject you, and when that happens, don't be surprised. It is just another in a long (and important) list of emotional responses that people experience under stress. Treat it as such.

Anger

Anger is a natural reaction to a perceived injustice. Hostility can sometimes be misdirected toward the minister of care. If this happens, you have to find out why the person is angry, determine what the anger means and decide what to do in this situation. Sometimes, the angry person is simply blowing off steam. Other times, the angry person is venting real hostility toward you. In either case, you can acknowledge the anger without becoming a target. You may say, gently, "I hear anger in your voice. Has something happened that I need to be aware of?" If you let yourself become a target for the anger, you run the risk of being hurt or getting angry yourself—which will not help the situation. Allow the angry person to speak directly to you. Don't assume anything.

Anger can be healing. If people don't address their anger and finish it, they will not be free to open themselves to healing and love. Be a safe person for patients to express their anger with; let those you visit say whatever they want to say. Their words won't hurt you. Going through their anger and coming out on the other side will free them.

Errors

All of us make mistakes. Many of our mistakes, glaring to us, will never be noticed by others. Even if they are noticed, they may not make a big difference. Errors can always be repaired.

The psychiatrist Rudolf Dreikurs' most famous dictum was, "Have the courage to be imperfect." We too often expect too much of our merely human selves. We can set up expectations that crush us, hurt us and burden us. Laugh at your mistakes, learn from them, even learn to like them — but don't try to rid yourself of any possibility of them. Ministers of care are human beings, and by definition, human beings are imperfect.

Chapter 10

Pain

Hippocrates said, "It is just as important to know what sort of person has a disease as to know what sort of disease a person has." In our ministry, we can be surrounded by disease, discouragement and disfigurement. But our ministry is about people. And people in pain are in need.

Some ministers of care will be visiting people in hospitals. Hospitals can be very painful places, not just physically, but also spiritually, mentally and emotionally. Though many healthcare professionals strive to treat their patients as complete persons, their primary responsibility is for the body. And sometimes bodies need to have needles put into them, electrodes attached, tests performed.

Furthermore, those entering the hospital have their closest possessions taken away — their clothes, their jewelry, their teeth, their glasses, their purse, their wallet. They are left with a hospital gown. They are usually surrounded by strangers who are in various stages of illness. Almost everyone who enters a hospital is afraid. They are afraid of what is happening and what might happen. They are filled with memories of what has happened to relatives or friends — perhaps even to themselves.

A minister of care needs to understand pain.

Pain is real. When people are in pain, there is no denying their discomfort. No matter what you hear, no matter what you believe, always assume that the person's pain is real.

Pain is personal. A person's pain and response to that pain are deeply personal. The pain exists within the person's own physical body and his or her response is unique.

Pain is a subjective experience. Only the patient can define what she or he is feeling. Respect the patient's description. Don't talk about your own pain.

Pain can reassure. Strange as it may seem, pain can reassure some people that what they expected is indeed happening on schedule. This belief may make their pain easier to bear. It has been said that one of the greatest pleasures in life is feeling that we are right. When the pain is what we thought it would be, we certainly are right!

Pain can be momentary or it can go on as if without end. Bursts of pain can shock the senses and leave a person shattered. Unalleviated and seemingly unending pain tests endurance. Such pain causes intense concentration and loneliness.

Pain can provoke fear. Many people fear pain, even to the point of avoiding making an appointment with the dentist. What fear must the pain of surgery or cancer cause, even in the most courageous?

The fear of pain is not always related to the physical pain itself. Anticipated pain can be as terrifying as actual pain. The mix of the physical and the psychological can be hard to communicate and hard for a visitor to understand. The pain caused by fear can be relentless. When lab results won't be back for days, when the specialist is out of town, when the technology is incomprehensible to the patient, when loved ones are struggling — people want someone who can help calm their fears.

Disease causes dis-ease. All ill health is stressful in ways that are unique to each individual. For some people, the worst part of illness is fear, for others it is the financial strain and for others, illness represents failure. Each person's dis-ease and disease is unique. As a minister of care, bring yourself to the ministry — not your preconceptions.

What Not to Say

What is pain like for you? From a stomachache to a toothache, from a splinter in your finger to something that requires hospitalization — you know something about physical pain. And you know pain that is spiritual and emotional. You know what pain is like for you, and you know how difficult it is to communicate it to someone else. And you know that what people in pain often need most is someone to be there with them and say, "I'm here for you." People in pain don't need to hear:

"It can't be that bad, can it?"
"Don't worry, everything will work out."

"I know what you are going through."
"I had that operation once, too."
"My doctor disagrees."
"I've had a really bad day."

Suffering is made more tolerable through caring. This caring, this acceptance is an important part of the ministry of care.

Talking about Pain

Act like what Chicago psychologist Robert Powers calls "a dumb nut": Don't assume anything. Let the other person go into as much detail or as little as they want to. Stay conversationally with them — don't get ahead of them. Be a good (and gentle) question-asker: If it seems that the person wants to talk, ask gentle questions to draw them out. Err on the side of respect. Probe only as far as the other person wants to go.

Seek the differences and uniquenesses of the person's experience. If you've had an experience similar to that of the person you are visiting, look for aspects of their experience that that are different from your own — then venture into the conversation further in those areas.

Look for the good. Encourage along the way (see pages 20 – 21). Remember that sometimes silence or gestures are good responses. Use all of your skills.

Vital Don'ts and Do's

When you are working with people who are in pain, remember:

Don't touch without permission. We can never know what hurts. Keep the appropriate distance. Let your eyes do the touching.

Don't prescribe. Even if you are a medical professional, as a minister of care your only job is prayerful presence, not diagnosis or prescription. Even if you are asked, refer the patient to the doctor or family.

Don't suggest. Never pass out advice.

Don't lecture. If you talk for more than twenty or thirty seconds at a time, you are probably saying too much. Ask, don't tell.

Don't back away. Pain can be ugly. Let your eyes reflect love and not disgust. When you see the ugly or the grossly painful, look steadfastly in one eye and then the other, and see Jesus in the one suffering.

Don't try to make it all better. Give the suffering person the unique and beautiful experience of simply being with them.

These things are not easy. No one likes to see another suffer. Remember that your ministry is all about prayerful presence. We must help healing happen with our Christ-like presence:

Do show your natural warmth. Use your enthusiasm, your humor, your reverence and respect, your personality, your eyes. Use whatever God has given you. Use your natural gifts and use them abundantly.

Do care. The old adage "People don't care how much you know until they know how much you care" is very true in the ministry of care. When you care, and people know it, you are almost there.

Do become appropriately close. Emotionally, physically and mentally, be aware of how close is close enough. Never get so close that you make the other person uncomfortable. It is better to err on the side of distance. However, be aware that people do want closeness. Sometimes moving your chair just half an inch closer makes people feel that you can be trusted.

Do show understanding. Use the five R's of listening (pages 17–20) to let the other person know that you understand.

Do respect the other person. This is the greatest gift you can give someone who is in pain. Remember to excuse yourself whenever the doctor or nurse comes into the room for an examination or consultation. Say it out loud. "I'll step out for a few minutes, Mr. Green. I'll be back when the doctor is finished. Is that all right with you?"

Be alert to signs of fatigue and end the visit a bit too early rather than a bit too late. The Russian psychologist Zigarnek observed that people are more likely to want to repeat an activity when they are stopped while they were enjoying it rather than later. Make your visits follow the Zigarnek effect.

Remember the person in your daily prayer. Make sure that the parish does, too.

Chapter 11

Special Cases

The special cases in this chapter are presented for two reasons. First, when you know a little about what other people are going through, you gain an appreciation of their situation and can better establish a caring rapport. When you know more, you're able to do more. Second and perhaps more importantly, when you know more about these situations, you'll understand yourself better: your own reactions, feelings and thoughts. Ministers of care who know themselves are the best visitors because they can trust themselves in different situations.

Situations like the ones described in this chapter can make anyone uncomfortable. They raise questions like these:

Will I know what to say?
What if I make a mistake?
Will we be able to communicate?
Can I get past physical appearances?
What help will I be?

These questions can guide you. Reverend John Hoffman suggests that we allow ourselves to move from humiliation toward humbleness. When we are fearful of how we'll do, we fear humiliation. When we open ourselves to being humbled (by our limitations, by the mystery of another's suffering) then we can become partners on a journey.

This is precisely what people in the following situations need — a partner on a journey, a companion. That is part of your ministry. You are there to help establish community with them. And in the sharing of community they will have an opportunity to grow.

Many of these people and their families are already further along in their journey. They are moving from grief to growth in a process that can either humiliate or humble the best of us. Be as open as you can be with these people. They have stories and wisdom to share.

Although you will use many of the skills in your ministry on a regular basis, there will be certain extraordinary situations that require special skills. Reread parts of this chapter as the need arises.

Terminal Illness

Some people know that their cancer will almost certainly kill them within a certain number of weeks or months, or that their child will die without an organ donor, or that an older relative is going to die soon because a weakened heart can't take much more. Terminal illness brings unique reactions from people. Much has been written about the stages of dying. Reading and knowing that information can be helpful.

But caution is necessary: Do not expect textbook principles to fit all people. You may recognize certain stages in a person who is dying, but never attempt to fit the patient into a theoretical pattern. Rather, attempt to enter the world of the patient and so gain an understanding of what this time is like for him or her. This holds true of ministry with the dying person's family. Approach the situation as if you are a blank piece of paper to be written on. The family writes on you, tells you their story, their particular situation. What is it like for them? Your job is not to provide solutions but rather presence and prayer.

Sudden Death

Imagine the shock of hearing of the sudden death of someone you know or love. Pastoral departments in hospitals in the United States say that, under normal circumstances, people generally need at least 72 hours to begin to prepare for the death of a loved one. When death comes gradually, people have a chance to say what they need to say, to think what they need to think, to pray what they need to pray. But automobile accidents, instantaneous heart attacks, murders: These situations do not provide that time. This has important implications for the minister of care. Perhaps survivors will need to tell you the things that they now cannot say to the person who has suddenly died. For the survivors, the shock of the death and the shock of having to make funeral arrangements can be overwhelming.

Sudden death can also produce sudden and intense anger. This anger can be directed at the deceased, at God, the police, frequently at the medical professionals involved. Remember to do your ministry: Listen with full attention and be there for them.

Suicide and Survivors

The shock that accompanies this kind of death is long-lasting. The care required for the family needs to be long-lasting also. Some reading may help you understand more about this form of tragedy, but you need not be an expert. Remember that there are survivors who grieve and who need your presence.

People will ask you about the church's teachings on suicide, and perhaps whether the one who has committed suicide can "go to heaven." Here's how Reverend Richard Prendergast summed it up during the homily for Larry, who died of suicide:

> Gone from our religious practice is the arrogance that overruled the mercy of God in deciding who was buried from church. That Larry took his own life is a great tragedy. That any of us might apply moral judgment to that tragedy would only be self-serving — and a clear violation of the Lord's command to love. The reality is that that could be any one of us resting in this casket this morning.
>
> A special word for those tempted to the same situation: If your life has become so difficult that you can no longer bear it, if your despair has so intensified that each hour is a burden, do not bear that burden alone. Reach out for help. It isn't necessary for us to get everything right, to do everything perfectly. All that is needed is to trust in one another.
>
> In God's name, let Larry rest in peace and let our concern be for the care and love of each other.

For some good prayers to offer with survivors, see the appendix, "Prayers for Particular Situations," in the 1989 *Order of Christian Funerals*. These prayers reflect the church's spirit of understanding and compassion for this most difficult situation.

Someone in a Coma

Occasionally you may visit someone who is in a coma. In this case, your work will mostly consist of prayer, although you may also be asked to visit with the family. If, in your regular check-in with the nurses' station, you learn that the patient is in a coma, it is still appropriate to visit, even if the family is not there.

When visiting a person in a coma or speaking to other people in the room, be very clear about who you are, why you are there and what you are doing. People in coma may retain their sense of hearing. Help the person to follow the action in the room by saying things aloud: "I'm going to pray a psalm from this beautiful prayerbook that I brought."

Never say anything in front of a person in a coma that you would not say to the person if he or she were fully aware. People have come out of a coma remembering things that people said. It is respectful and medically correct to speak to comatose people as if they could hear you. Never underestimate how important this may be to the person.

With the families and friends of those in a coma, quiet and patient listening is called for. Comas are torture for families. They are unable to communicate with the person and they fear the worst even as they hope for the best.

Surgery and Intensive Care

The minister of care is more likely to be involved with the family than the patient during and immediately after surgery. Visiting hours in the intensive care unit are usually limited, and often only family members are permitted to visit.

You are needed with the family. You probably won't have to say very much. It is a time of waiting. Don't feel self-conscious. Your presence is noticed and will be appreciated. Be calm, composed and available. Try to resist the temptation to scurry from one person to another, getting coffee, making light conversation. This is a hard time for any family member — and for the minister of care.

Disabilities

Frequently, ministers of care encounter people who are disabled. The people you visit may have lost sight, hearing, speech, use of limbs, the limbs themselves or control over bodily functions. It is important to remember that people with a disability are *people* with a disability.

What do you see first?

The wheelchair?

The physical problem?

The person?

If you saw a person in a wheelchair unable to get up the stairs into a building, would you say "there is a handicapped person unable to find a ramp"? Or would you say "there is a person with a disability who is handicapped by an inaccessible building"?

What is the proper way to speak to or about someone who has a disability?

Consider how you would introduce someone — Jane Doe — who doesn't have a disability. You would give her name, where she lives, what she does or what she is interested in: She likes swimming, or eating Mexican food, or watching Robert Redford movies.

Why say it differently for a person with disabilities? Every person is made up of many characteristics — mental as well as physical — and few want to be identified only by their ability to play tennis or by their love for fried onions or by the mole that's on their face. Those are just parts of us.

In speaking or writing, remember that children or adults with disabilities are like everyone else — except they happen to have a disability. Therefore, here are a few tips for improving your language related to disabilities and handicaps.

1. Speak of the person first, then the disability.

2. Emphasize abilities, not limitations.

3. Do not label people as part of a disability group — don't say "the disabled"; say "people with disabilities."

4. Don't give excessive praise or attention to a person with a disability; don't patronize them.

5. Choice and independence are important; let the person do or speak for himself or herself as much as possible; if addressing an adult, say "Bill" instead of "Billy."

6. A *disability* is a functional limitation that interferes with a person's ability to walk, hear, talk, learn, etc.; use *handicap* to describe a situation or barrier imposed by society, the environment or oneself.

Say...	*Instead of...*
child with a disability	disabled or handicapped child
person with cerebral palsy	palsied, or C.P., or spastic
person who is deaf or hard of hearing	deaf and dumb
person with retardation	retarded
person with epilepsy or person with seizure disorder	epileptic
person who has ...	afflicted, suffers from, victim
without speech, nonverbal	mute, or dumb
developmental delay	slow
emotional disorder or mental illness	crazy or insane
uses a wheelchair	confined to a wheelchair
with Down Syndrome	mongoloid
has a learning disability	is learning disabled
nondisabled	normal, healthy
has a physical disability	crippled
congenital disability	birth defect
condition	disease (unless it is a disease)
seizures	fits
cleft lip	hare lip
mobility impaired	lame
medically involved or has chronic illness	sickly
paralyzed	invalid or paralytic
has hemiplegia (paralysis of one side of the body)	hemiplegic
has quadriplegia (paralysis of both arms and legs)	quadriplegic
has paraplegia (loss of function in lower body only)	paraplegic
of short stature	dwarf or midget
accessible parking	handicapped parking

Think of the person first and your words will follow. For example, think of and refer to the child or adult as a person with epilepsy, a person who has an emotional disorder or mental illness, a person who is deaf or hearing-impaired, someone who uses a wheelchair, rather than an "epileptic," a "schizophrenic," a "deaf-mute" or a "cripple."

It may be helpful to ask questions such as, "How long have you been without the use of your legs?" "When did you first lose your sight?" "Can you hear me now?" "May I help you down the hall?" or "Would you like me to call the nurse to assist you?" Such questions recognize the person's disability and may help to put both of you at ease.

Sometimes the person will give you an opening to ask questions. "Well, I just don't feel like my old self since the operation." "I'm having a hard time walking with this cane." "I'm not in here for paralysis. I've had that for a year." "I don't see you very well because they are working on my eye. I may not have my vision for very long." "I can't seem to say the words I'm thinking anymore." Such recognition comments are for you to notice. When people volunteer information, they expect you to ask a follow-up question. If you don't, it can seem as if you aren't listening or that you don't care.

People who are disabled sometimes feel strongly about doing things things by themselves. Be sensitive to this. When you want to help someone, ask first if it is all right to help. If they say no, let it go. They want to do it themselves, even though it may take longer and they may feel worse. Simply be patient.

Alcoholism and Drug Abuse

These are two rampant diseases in our culture. When you visit someone who has been hospitalized for these problems, be sensitive of your role as a parish representative who physically communicates the support of the local faith community. Don't get caught up in the therapy, or in the experiences that you or your family may have had with alcoholism or drug addiction. Simply see it as a disease, a condition, a medical problem. Then you can be a minister of care ready to listen and be open.

Psychological Problems

Occasionally you may be called upon to visit a patient in a psychiatric ward. Part of your preparation for the visit will be to dismiss any preconceived notions about insanity and mental wards. Remember that this person is hurting emotionally in a way similar to the patient who is hurting physically. After your preparation, treat it as a normal visit. Find out about visiting hours, and consult with the nurses in charge before you visit. You may be asked to call the doctor for permission to visit.

Birth of a Baby

This can be a fun visit, but not always. Don't bring any assumptions to this visit. Instead, find out what it is like for the new parents. This is not a time to speak of your children, your delivery, your advice on parenting. It is a time for prayer, parish greetings and good wishes. Be alert for concerns, cares or stresses that new life can bring to a couple or family.

When a baby is born prematurely, ill or with a disability, fear is a dominant feeling. In such a situation, let the parents talk, cry or be silent as they wish during your visit. Visit more than once, at short intervals, so they can trust in your presence. Visit the baby, too. Pray.

Visiting Professionals

Don't be intimidated if you are called upon to visit medical professionals, clergy or religious who are ill. These people are afraid too. Sometimes they are at a real disadvantage because they know too much! Treat them as you would anyone else. Avoid "I'm doing your job" jokes or comments. Often we overlook the real human needs that these people have. Use your training — you are the minister for them.

Amputation or Disfigurement

Amputation of an arm or a leg, removal of a breast or a bodily organ, partial or total paralysis, or disfiguring injury is an experience of major loss. It can threaten a person's self-image and sense of self-worth. A person who has gone through such a loss knows that his or her body will never be the same; the lost function can never be entirely replaced. Besides physical pain, such a loss can cause great emotional trauma. Some people find themselves unable to cope with such change, and mourn the loss without moving to acceptance of it. A person may withdraw into depression, and may refuse to enter fully into the rehabilitation process.

Most people respond to disfigurement with grief, depression and anxiety. Moving toward acceptance depends on the person's ability to handle loss and crisis. Coping with such emotional trauma depends on the person's readiness to express their feelings about the loss. A skilled minister of care will listen "between the lines," allowing the person to name their feelings of denial, anger, frustration, depression, sadness or guilt, helping the person to move through these to acceptance and willingness to continue with life.

Spouses and other close family members may need some care in working through their feelings when a loved one has undergone amputation or disfigurement. Family members will need support as they cope with the changes in their lives. You may want to form a team of ministers of care to assist in the support needed by the patient as well as family members.

Allowing family members to express their feelings of anger, being overly burdened, or even guilt is important if the family is to begin to accept the changes that come with amputation or disfigurement.

Grieving the loss of a body part takes time. It is comparable to the experience of bereavement that follows the death of a loved one. Providing ongoing ministry to the patient and to family members can help the entire family adjust to the changes that accompany such major loss. You can assist in ongoing support for the patient and family by making available information about local support groups. Hospital social workers are good sources of this kind of information.

Dementia

Dementia affects only a minority of older people. As dementia begins to develop, changes occur in a person's behavior that can be frightening, not only for the person, but for family members and friends. You may visit a person in their home or in a nursing home who forgets events, names and places, repeats questions, has difficulty finding words to communicate, or gets lost in familiar surroundings. Such changes can be symptoms of a form of dementia.

In ministering to persons with dementia, it is important to remember that dementia affects communication in a variety of ways. Understanding these changes and learning new ways to communicate will help to make your visits more meaningful. Reintroducing yourself each time you visit will help the person to know who you are and why you are there. Simply say something like, "Hello, Miss Brown. My name is Marilyn Jones; I'm from St. Catherine. The parish is concerned about you and has sent me to visit with you."

It is helpful to remember the basic skills of communication: establish eye contact before speaking, allow enough time for a response, make use of appropriate touch, and be aware of the tone and volume of your voice, your facial expression and body language. Be aware of how the person is responding to you; this may be different from your last visit. Be warm and open to the person's concerns. At times it is sufficient simply to let the person know that you care and that you are with him or her.

Many people with dementia are aware of their memory loss and their inability to communicate as well as they once did. A person who has dementia may need to talk about the changes he or she is noticing and want to share what is happening to them. Listen patiently to the person who has difficulty finding the words to describe his or her feelings. Helping with words is beneficial. Often, simply repeating or restating the person's thought will let the person know that you understood, even though the person is not fully able to communicate. Naming the feeling the person is expressing is very important in supporting the emotional needs of the person with dementia, and can go a long way in helping the person's quality of life. Be careful to listen first. Don't anticipate every response. Be patient. Let the person try as hard as he or she wishes to before you try to respond.

From early in life, people know what it is to be loved; they know the loneliness of not having someone to care for them. These feelings are stored in long-term memory and are experienced even in the late stages of dementia. Many people with dementia respond to the religious symbols and rituals they knew as children. Memories that connect with a person's spirituality may be touched in a variety of ways:

- Listening to classical music, favorite hymns or music of the person's culture.

- Listening to or repeating familiar prayers or scripture passages.

- Visiting the chapel or local parish church.

- Watching television programs about nature, animal life and little children.
- Taking a walk out in nature.

A person with dementia may be living in a different time, and may re-experience old grief and loss from a time when a significant person in his or her life died. Rather than trying to remind the person of the passage of time, it is more helpful to acknowledge the person's sadness and loss. A skilled minister of care can move from one "time zone" to another with few discernible cues.

To help the person with dementia deal with anger and diminished self-worth, listen with respect, assist the person in naming feelings and respond in ways that allow the person to say more, to cry or to reflect silently.

How do you pray with a person who has dementia? Ordinarily, with people in the early stages of dementia, you pray as you would with any person you visit as a minister of care. With people in the severe stages of dementia, praying for the person, quietly or aloud, is appropriate. Pray familiar prayers such as the Our Father, another prayer that the person has prayed throughout life (ask a family member or friend if there is such a prayer) or one of the prayers in PCS. Familiar prayers can be very comforting for the person with dementia.

Dementia indicates physical deterioration in more than one area of a person's brain. There are several different causes of dementia, including Alzheimer's disease, multi-infarct dementia caused by small strokes, Parkinson's disease, Huntington's disease and progressive aphasia.

Alzheimer's Disease

The most common cause of dementia is Alzheimer's disease. The cause or causes of this form of dementia is still unknown. Although there is currently no cure for Alzheimer's, some symptoms can be treated. Symptoms progress over time, but they vary greatly from one person to another.

A person in the early stages of Alzheimer's disease may feel more comfortable with small groups of family members and friends in familiar sur-roundings. Persons with Alzheimer's are often aware of their impaired memory and are fearful of embarrassing themselves in larger groups. However, people with mild impairment are still able to enjoy many activities. It is important to focus on the person's remaining abilities instead of emphasizing any impairments.

As the disease advances, the person may become frustrated and depressed. Emotional swings may occur. If this happens while you are visiting, remember that this behavior is due to the dementia, and is not the conscious choice of the person. Being peaceful in your movements and in your inner self can make a difference in the mood of the moment. Redirecting the person's focus to something other than their frustration or depression can help to change the frame of mind.

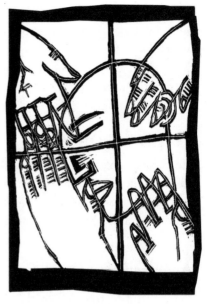

Parkinson's Disease

People with Parkinson's disease lack a substance in their central nervous systems that controls muscle activity. Typical of this disease are tremors, stiffness and motor difficulties. Some people with Parkinson's disease may develop dementia as the condition progresses. Motor difficulties associated with the disease can be treated with certain drugs, but they have no effect on any dementia that may exist.

Lou Gehrig's Disease (ALS)

Amyotrophic lateral sclerosis destroys muscle tissue. This disease, with no known cause or cure, will bring death in two to five years. Thirty thousand Americans have this disease. It weakens every function in the body. Some people with ALS cannot move or speak. "I'm adapting to what little I have left," says Dick Bergeron of Exton, Pennsylvania, who has this disease. "As long as I can talk, I can live. I can live with all the machines. I can live with all the psychological barriers. If I can communicate, I can focus on that." Ministers of care try to communicate.

Huntington's Disease

Huntington's disease is a hereditary disorder characterized by irregular and involuntary movements of arms, legs and facial muscles, as well as progressive dementia. People with this disease may also experience psychiatric problems. To learn how best to minister to a person with Huntington's disease, you will probably find it very helpful to consult the person's nurses, doctors and family members. The more you know about the person and the specific condition, the better.

Progressive Aphasia

Progressive aphasia is a rare brain disorder involving a gradual loss of the ability to speak and write, while the memory may remain intact. Some people with this disorder develop symptoms of dementia, while others may not display any other symptom except the loss of their ability to speak.

Acquired Immunodeficiency Syndrome (AIDS)

"Ministering to people with AIDS provides a unique opportunity to walk with those who are suffering, to be compassionate toward those whom we might otherwise fear, to bring strength and courage both to those who face the prospect of dying as well as to their loved ones."

— *The Many Faces of AIDS: A Gospel Response*, National Conference of Catholic Bishops (1987)

In their document, the bishops of the United States list some facts about the AIDS disease:

• AIDS is a disease for which there is at present no cure.

• AIDS is a disease that cuts across all racial and ethnic lines.

• AIDS is a disease that afflicts children, including infants and toddlers, as well as adults.

After extensive research, there is no evidence that AIDS can be contracted through ordinary casual contact. AIDS can be contracted through certain forms of intimate sexual contact and encounters with tainted blood. It can also be transmitted from a mother to her child during pregnancy as well as by artificial insemination or organ transplants.

Persons with AIDS, their families and their friends need solidarity, comfort and support as they face the inevitability of death and go through the emotions connected with it. Ministering to people with AIDS requires that the minister be comfortable in the relationship. If you find that you are not at ease visiting a person with AIDS, it is important that you tell your coordinator so that another minister can assume this particular ministry.

You can be of great help to the person with AIDS and especially his or her family members and friends when you can provide accurate information to dispel confusion and allay fears. Your coordinator can help you find this information; also, the chaplain at your local hospital will have helpful material available.

The reality of AIDS means that family members may have to confront choices and situations beyond their control. A mixture of painful emotions and reactions may cause unnecessary tensions. These tensions, in turn, can build up walls of loneliness between the very persons who could support one another the most.

You may find that you are able to help the patient and family members build bridges among themselves simply by freeing them to talk about their feelings. You may gently encourage them to be more direct and open with one another, thus giving them an opportunity to put into words what their fears and worries are.

Recognition of the significant presence of people who are not members of the biological family is often important to the well-being of the patient. The skilled minister of care makes no judgments, but is simply present, modeling understanding, compassion and acceptance.

The celebration of the anointing of the sick in the early stages of the disease, as well as in the later stages, can strengthen the faith and courage of the person with AIDS and family and friends, providing inner healing to all involved. You may want to consult with your coordinator or parish priest about ways in which the parish community can join in the celebration of the sacrament.

A Final Thought

Earlier we recommended that you consult with the family and medical staff to learn how to minister effectively with people who have particular diseases. This is to be preferred over library research or your own experience, because it focuses on the person you are visiting, not on the disease. The person always comes first.

Additional Resources

AIDS

Called to Compassion and Responsibility: A Response to the HIV/AIDS Crisis.

AIDS/HIV Hotline: 1-800-CDC-INFO

Here are some local support services in Illinois:

AIDS Foundation of Chicago
200 West Jackson Boulevard, Suite 2200
Chicago IL 60606
Illinois Perinatal HIV Hotline: 1-800-439-4079

Kane County Health Department
1240 N. Highland Avenue
Aurora IL 60506
630-208-3801

Illinois AIDS Hotline: 1-800-243-AIDS or 1-800-782-0423 (TDD)

Alzheimer's Disease

The Alzheimer's Association
225 N. Michigan Avneue, Floor 17
Chicago, IL 60601-7633

The Alzheimer's Disease Education and Referral Center
P.O. Box 8250
Silver Spring MD 20907-8257
1-800-438-4380

Disabilities

You may find that the people you visit need to learn about civil rights or services for people with disabilities. This information is available from

National Council on Disability
1331 F. Street NW, Suite 850
Washington DC 20004, 202-272-2004

For pastoral services such as religious education, accessible church buildings and the like, consult your diocesan directory.

Parkinson's Disease

Parkinson's Disease Foundation
1359 Broadway, Suite 1509
New York NY 10018
212-923-4478
Toll-free Helpline: 800-457-6676

American Parkinson's Disease Information and Referral Center
Central DuPage Hospital
25 North Winfield Road
Winfield IL 60190
Coordinator: Sarah Stukas, 847-657-5787, 800-223-9776

APDA (American Parkinson's Disease Association)
135 Parkinson Avenue
Staten Island, NY 10305
2800-233-2732, 718-981-8001

Chapter 12

Your Own Life

As a minister of care, you will be dealing with other people's problems and difficulties. In the ministry of care, you deal with the negatives of life: illness, death, discouragement and loss. This can take its toll on your life at home, but it is not the only effect of your ministry. You need to be conscious of the impact that your ministry will have on your own life. The times that you share with the sick and elderly, important as they are, are times when you are away from your own family and friends. You will be distracted from their concerns. You will have concerns and worries and joys that your family cannot fully share.

It is sometimes easier to love strangers than to love the people who are closest to you. Loving strangers does not require the same commitment, the same knowledge or even the same skills as loving people who are closest. It can be very discouraging to the people who live with you that you sometimes find more fulfillment and success in ministering to strangers than in caring for your own family.

Do you spend enough time with your spouse and your children? Many people believe that the quality of the time spent with family is more important than the quantity. But it is vital to acknowledge how much time you do need with each member of your family, as well as how much quality needs to be within that quantity of time. If you are not careful, you may be fooled into thinking that a few minutes of "quality time" with everyone together will make up for the time that you are away. Spend enough time with each person.

How do ministers of care keep their lives from getting too complicated? Successful ministers of care can balance the stresses of their own lives with the stresses of the people they visit. They have certain strategies, values and tips that can be useful.

Dr. Richard Westley suggests that we adopt a personal motto. "Do what love requires" is his. Develop your own motto. It can help you direct yourself in times of stress at home and away from home.

Management expert Peter Drucker advises, "Do first things first, second things hardly ever." Agendas have a way of growing beyond limits. Always set priorities. All the things that need to get done don't get done on the same day, but the important things will always be taken care of because they are the first things.

Author Alan Lakein writes, "Plan your work and then work your plan." Work goes faster if we take time to plan it in some detail. If we get lost, at least we have a road map. Planning also helps to eliminate what is not necessary. This is true for your ministry of care as well. Good preparation will make much better visits.

Reverend George Kane recommends, "People before things." This cardinal rule is hard to follow, but can be a life-saver when we are confused about what to do next.

Balance

Here are some tips to help you balance this ministry with your family life.

Align goals. Bring your spouse and your family into your ministry by letting them know what you do, when you do it and why you do it. With this knowledge, they can align their support and expectations.

Connect with your family before and after your visits. Don't discuss who you visited or what you talked about (that information is confidential) but simply be present to your family. They need you too.

Include your family in your training and in your reading. Make sure you include them in your prayer life.

Communicate often, especially when schedules in your household get hectic. In person, by phone, with notes or on the family calendar, let everyone know what is happening.

Seek cooperation and agreement. If there is disagreement, try to work it out so that everyone is satisfied with the solution.

Never underestimate the value of a sincere compliment. Let your family know how much you appreciate their support.

And remember: Your ministry of care is part time. Home is full time.

Chapter 13

Evaluating Your Ministry

When you evaluate your work, do so with the proper perspective. On one hand, helping people in need can feel very good. As a helper, you can exaggerate your influence. It is not enough to evaluate your ministry according to the good feelings you get from it. On the other hand, ministers of care often visit people who don't get better. In situations of chronic illness and death, it is easy to evaluate yourself as ineffective and of no use. Both these extremes miss the point of the ministry.

Professional ministers are careful and realistic in evaluating their effectiveness. They know from experience that ministry can't easily be quantified, but before measuring progress, it is necessary to decide what this progress should be going toward. There has to be a goal.

People in business have used written goals for many years. They begin their work with a deliberate aim: the end point. These goals have been called "dreams with deadlines." Ministers of care can do very much the same thing. Carefully and prayerfully decide what you want to happen. You may want to be a helpful listener, a resource person, a prayerful partner, a family companion or a timely visitor. Any of these can be chosen as personal goals.

To know where you are going is essential, and so is the recognition of who you are — the gift. It is important to recognize precisely what you have to offer. Perhaps you are lively, interesting, spiritual, happy, calm, accepting, patient — perhaps you exemplify any of the deep and important qualities that make up a person who is a gift. You have to know who you are (a gift) and where you are going (a goal).

The link between the gift and the goal is the guiding line. The guiding line consists of all the little daily activities that help you to be a gift to others and move you toward achieving your goal. When you feel scattered, it may be that your less important activities are not leading toward your larger goal. If this is the case, you'll feel off center because you are not as focused as you could be. Remember your larger goal, and give yourself a chance to do what is important to do.

If you feel uncomfortable making a particular visit, it may be that you are trying to minister as someone else does, instead of recognizing and using your own particular gift. It's fine to use the examples set by good ministers you've known, but the key to good ministry is making your own contribution.

Self-Evaluation

It is essential that you evaluate your ministry. However, it is rare to receive direct, overt feedback that you can use in your evaluation. Here are some hints.

Begin with the end in mind. What do you want your ministry to "look like" when it is done well? Form a clear picture, a clear target, in your mind and it will be easier to evaluate.

Recognize, name and understand your greatest natural strength. When you understand it, whether it is making conversation, being reliable, being empathetic or whatever your particular gift may be, then you can continuously exercise it.

Do the same with your greatest need. Don't fear your weaknesses. Once you name them, you can begin to improve upon them. Does your family know what your fears and concerns about visiting the sick may be? When you talk to another minister of care, a friend or family member about them, you can discover assets that can help you improve.

After each visit, ask yourself: How did I use my strengths to minister? How did I improve just a little?

Stay in touch with other ministers of care. A regular monthly reflection session can make a big difference. Other ministers can be human mirrors and resources, offering the encouragement of peers.

Take delight in your ministry. Let it be a joy. If it becomes burdensome or boring, take a break from it. If it isn't fulfilling, don't continue with it for now.

Chapter 14

Conclusion

A minister of care must be a person who cares. The person who cares is one who is present to another, especially in times of pain, loss and stress. To share life's struggles with another, to articulate the prayer that emanates from the groaning of the Spirit within, to celebrate the dying and rising of the Lord in the concrete reality of people's lives — all this makes a difference.

Becoming a caring person is a lifelong process. In some ways, you are always beginning. You are always growing and deepening your perceptions and sensitivities. A minister of care needs a hunger for life, a thirst for healing. This hunger and thirst somehow rise from a relationship with the Lord that is always becoming more conscious, more active and more alive. To foster this process of growth, attend to the following needs.

Deepen your own spirituality, your way of looking at life and coping with life's struggles and challenges in the pattern of Jesus.

Care for yourself. Listen to yourself in times of stress, in active moments as well as calm moments.

Obtain formation and reflection on a regular basis. Participating in monthly reflection sessions with a competent supervisor of ministers of care, reading, sharing experiences of ministry, programs designed for ministers of care and the like will help you to grow in your ministry.

Be affirmed as a minister of care. For the minister of care to have an official mandate from the bishop of the diocese says, "I am good enough to do this and the church recognizes this."

Be accountable; that is, know that you count. Be aware of common mistakes and, if you find that you are making them, correct them: for instance, cheering up a patient rather than being present to their pain, offering sympathy rather than empathy, passive listening rather than active listening.

God loves you and chooses you to make concrete the reality of the divine love for all humankind. Go forth knowing you do not go alone. Go with Jesus Christ.

I cannot believe that the purpose of life is to be happy. I think the purpose of life is to be useful, to be responsible, to be compassionate. It is, above all, to matter, to count, to stand for something, to have made some difference that you lived at all.

— *Leo Rosten*

A Structure for the Ministry of Care

In a time when society's attitude toward the sick and the dying is marked by indifference and abandonment, and when euthanasia is considered by some to be merciful and humane, we need to ponder the healing ministry of Jesus who was gentle, compassionate and eager to touch those who came to him in faith. We need to remember once more that Jesus came not only to physically heal people, but also to bring sight to those unable to see the vision of God, to enable songs of praise to God, to bring new life to those whose spirits are withered by sin. This healing ministry of Jesus always happens in the context of human relationships.

It is with this healing power in mind that Jesus sent his followers to preach the reign of God and to heal the sick.

What can we learn from reflecting upon and praying over the gospel stories of Jesus' healing ministry? Why is the church called to be present to those who are sick and dying? What does this ministry look like in today's parish? How does the local community surround those who are sick and dying with an abundance of life and life-giving hope? How does parish leadership provide for the caring ministry of the sick? These questions precede the choices a local parish makes in shaping the parish ministry of care.

First Steps

How can a parish initiate, organize, train and provide for the development of a local ministry of care? Parish leaders should begin by identifying a person whose personal charism reflects the compassion and caring of Jesus, and who is willing to take on the responsibility for ministering to and with the ministers of care. Generosity of spirit, training in spirituality and a commitment to the ongoing formation of the ministers of care are especially important qualities in the person who takes on the responsibility for the development of this ministry. This person needs to have the qualities essential to any ministry and other capabilities as well: the abilities to do the necessary research, to create effective structures to support the ministry, to provide resources to enrich the ministers and to supervise the ministers regularly.

Research is the foundation of any successful outcome. The best initial research is talking to people who are already involved in this ministry in other parishes. Then consult the appropriate diocesan office. Find literature and other informational resources. Identify existing structures in the parish that could support the ministry, and find out how mutual support and cooperation could take place. In other words, collect the data and connect with people. Imagine what the ministry, in its fullness, will be like. Then make a list of what needs to be put in place to allow that to come into being.

Goals

Setting goals is the next step. In beginning this ministry, it is important to keep the goals simple, measurable and achievable. Here is an example.

The goal of our ministry of care is to provide presence, prayer and sacrament to parishioners who are hospitalized or homebound, and to residents of local nursing homes.

Once goals are set, the planning process moves to designing strategies for the implementation of the goals. Questions to be addressed include:

How can the parish be educated about this ministry?
Who will become ministers of care?
What basic commitments do the ministers need to make?
How will they be recruited and selected?
How and when will they be trained and formed?

How will they be mandated and commissioned?

How will we know if we are achieving our goals?

How will we evaluate the formation process?

Once we have begun, how will we provide for newcomers to this ministry?

How often will we gather to share and process our experience of this ministry?

How will we continue to grow as ministers?

Education of parish members not only alerts them to this ministry, but also helps create an openness to accepting lay ministers of care. It sets the stage for calling forth members who have the gifts of compassion and care. This education can take several forms: articles in the Sunday bulletin, announcements at Sunday Mass, dialogue with existing parish groups, parish staff commitment to the support of this ministry, or one-to-one visits with potential ministers.

Recruiting and Training

The selection of ministers is crucial. The coordinator invites potential ministers to enter discernment, and then interviews each person who responds. They discuss expectations, clarify roles and commitment, share vision and personal stories. Basic questions to be addressed during the interview include:

What is your personal experience of sickness and death, the elderly and the homebound?

Why are you interested in becoming a minister of care?

What are your expectations?

What gifts do you bring to this ministry?

To what area of this ministry do you feel called? That is, visits to people who are in hospitals, nursing homes, or homebound?

What is your availability for this ministry?

Before the interview concludes, the coordinator and prospective minister should both know clearly that the person has or has not been accepted into the ministry. There should be a clear commitment from the potential minister of care to the entire training program, to a specific amount of time to be spent in this ministry and to participation in the monthly reflection session with other ministers of care.

When all the potential ministers have been interviewed and all candidates selected, it is wise to call them together for an orientation session. At this session, the candidates meet one another and experienced ministers of care, if the group already exists. The orientation should provide information on the theology of ministry, allow the candidates to share their stories of responding to the ministry, allow them to hear some experiences of those who have been doing this work and offer them a chance to ask questions. Before concluding, all pray together.

The training program for the candidates may be provided by the diocese, the deanery or the parish. One diocesan-approved training program includes six two-hour sessions. It is outlined in the next section.

The content of the basic training sessions may vary depending on the knowledge that different individuals and groups bring to their new ministry. With some groups, all the elements listed below will need to be addressed; with others, only some of them. You may need to plan for more than one session for one or another of the topics. The decision to include some or all of the elements listed will depend upon the previous experience and background of the group. When in doubt, include all the topics, mentioning to the group that some of them will find the material a review.

Initial Formation

This is an example of a training program consisting of six parts.

1. Experience and Theology of Illness
A theology of illness and suffering
A theology of ministry for the sick
Biblical roots of healing
The tradition of the church in caring for the sick
The mission of the parish community to the sick and elderly
The call of all Christians to continue the healing ministry of Jesus Christ
The patient's experience of illness

2. Basic Skills of Visitation
Establishing a pastoral relationship
Style of pastoral visits
Communicating a climate of openness and trust
Active listening skills
Consistency, frequency and length of visits

Expectations and setting limits
Ministry to the patient/resident and family/friends
Methods of reflection on experiences
Getting in touch with one's own feelings

3. Theology of Pastoral Care of the Sick
A contemporary theology of church and sacrament
A contemporary understanding of the theology and spirituality of
    eucharist and the anointing of the sick
Understanding and using *Pastoral Care of the Sick: Rites of Anointing
    and Viaticum*
How to's and role playing: rite of communion of the sick
Pastoral sensitivity to the sacramental needs of the sick and elderly

4. Ministry to the Aging
Experience of aging
Responses to aging
Life review and search for meaning
Grieving losses in the context of faith
Coping with the present situation
Ministry to the aging
Confinement: home and nursing home

5. Death and Dying: Implications for the Minister
A theology of death and dying
Experience of loss throughout life
Right to die with dignity
The death experience: Being there
Stages of grief
Enabling people to grieve well
Walking with people who grieve

6. Prayer and Pastoral Visitation
A contemporary theology of spirituality
A contemporary understanding of how to pray in the name of the church
The pastoral place of prayer in ministry to the sick and elderly
Styles of prayer
When to pray, when not to pray aloud, how to pray, what to pray
Being a leader of prayer
Skills in leading spontaneous prayer
Personal reflection after each visit/journal keeping

When the training program is concluded, the ministers of care are publicly commissioned at Sunday Mass. Mandates, signed by the bishop and the pastor, are presented to the ministers; these indicate that the minister is called by the bishop to care for the sick and homebound. A bulletin announcement of the commissioning, listing the names of the new ministers, is a further step in the education of the parish and an affirmation of this ministry.

Ongoing Formation

Monthly reflection sessions provide a forum for ministers of care to share their experiences, process their feelings (which is especially important for ministers who work with terminally ill persons) and continue their development as ministers. These sessions are vital to the growth of all involved in the ministry. They are also an essential part in the ongoing supervision and evaluation of the ministry. Inability to participate regularly in these sessions is a serious obstacle to the fullness of this parish ministry.

Sample Formats for Monthly Meetings

Option A.

1. Gathering in a warm, friendly, welcoming space
2. Sharing led by coordinator or designated person
   Questions to evoke sharing:
   What are you learning?
   What do you need to learn?
   What has been your experience of ministry in the past month?
   What questions do you have about your ministry?
3. Break
4. Input from the coordinator on specific area previously requested
   by theministers
5. Closing prayer led by group member

Option B.

1. Gathering
2. Introduction of speaker for evening
3. Input on specific topic by speaker

4. Break
5. Group process/interaction on topic
6. Group response reported to speaker
7. Speaker response and wrap-up
8. Closing prayer

Option C.

1. Gathering
2. Sharing of experience of ministry
3. Break
4. Continued sharing of experience of ministry
5. Closing prayer

Topics for additional formation during reflection sessions might include ministry to the bereaved, ministry to children, spirituality of the minister, theology of sacrament, anointing of the sick, developing communication skills, role playing (visits to the sick, for example) and other concerns suggested by group members.

Each minister of care should be invited annually to evaluate his or her experience and commitment to the ministry. Evaluation meetings between individual ministers and the coordinator will need to be scheduled. Participation in the regular monthly reflection sessions is an important factor to be considered in the evaluation. After reflection and evaluation, the minister may then renew commitment for another year, or may choose to bring closure to this involvement.

Caring for the Coordinator

While caring for the ministers of care is a special responsibility for the coordinator, caring for the coordinator is just as important. This includes support structures that allow the coordinator to grow in responsibility for others, to invite others into the ministry, to develop skills of leadership and to maintain good order and integrity in this ministry. Such support can be found in gathering with other coordinators on a diocesan or deanery level. If no such network exists in a local area, start one! Call other coordinators together to share experiences, ideas and prayer. Do this regularly and it becomes a network of support.

Do more than belong — participate.
Do more than care — help.
Do more than believe — practice.
Do more than be fair — be kind.
Do more than forgive — forget.
Do more than dream — work.

—*William Arthur Ward*